The Art of SMILING

FINDING AND RELEASING YOUR *Heavenly Joy*

By Charlene Moorer

Board Certified Christian Counselor, NCC, LPC

The Art of Smiling: Finding and Releasing Your Heavenly Joy

Trilogy Christian Publishers
A Wholly Owned Subsidiary of Trinity Broadcasting Network
2442 Michelle Drive, Tustin, CA 92780

Trilogy Christian Publishing.
Trilogy Disclaimer: The views and content expressed in this book are those of the author and may not necessarily reflect the views and doctrine of Trilogy Christian Publishing or the Trinity Broadcasting Network.
10 9 8 7 6 5 4 3 2 1
Library of Congress Cataloging-in-Publication Data is available.
ISBN 979-8-89333-364-0
ISBN 979-8-89333-365-7 (ebook)

Scripture Base

"When anxiety was great within me, your consolation brought me joy"

(Psalm 94:19, NIV)

Quote

"The Promised Land always lies on the other side of a wilderness."

—Havelock Ellis

Dedication

I dedicate the book first to God. He is the author and finisher of my faith. And my faith in Him brings me heavenly joy. Then, to my family, by whom I am so greatly blessed for their support. Love you all more than words can express! Lastly, to my therapy participants and to everyone in need of joy, be encouraged; joy is not far from you. Just receive it by faith.

Foreword

Charlene Moorer is a treasured member of the church I pastor. It is with great confidence that I refer individuals to her counseling practice because I know that they will receive from Charlene's compassion, years of experience, clinical expertise, and counsel that is solidly based on the Word of God. I am so excited for you to read this book on the heavenly joy God has for you! It is full of truth that will set you free. As I read through it myself, it caused me to reflect back on my own life, to a time when I desperately needed to find true joy.

I remember sitting as an unsaved teenager in more than one high school class, being so disinterested and bored beyond belief that I would take out a sheet of paper and start doodling on it. Sometimes, I would write the words "I'm so bored," but the word that I wrote the most was "smile." Looking back on that, I think how odd it was for me, as an unsaved teen, to write the word "smile," a word that was so foreign to my existence. The only explanation that I can think of is that my spirit, although lost, was crying out for an elusive joy that, at that time, I didn't even know existed.

In my B.C. days, my life was characterized by acute depression. After receiving Jesus Christ as my Lord, although I experienced many ups and downs, especially in my early years in Christ, there was consistent peace and inner *joy* that stemmed out of the realization of and gratefulness for what Jesus had done for me. And that peace and joy were often reflected in a smile that I wore wherever I went. What a change in my characterization! Thank You, Jesus!

You are about to discover that there is *power* in your smile. Your smile can be anointed. The smile that is an outflow and result of heavenly *joy* brings *victory*, and you will find that there is a Spirit of Victory upon what you are about to read. God has given Charlene such mighty revelation on His *victorious joy* and how to access it by faith—no matter what circumstances you may be facing.

This book will give you the tools to not only see what the Lord has for you but also how to practically access that joy on purpose. You will learn how to live continually aware of the joy supply, and not just as an extra add-on to your life or a "wouldn't it be nice if" benefit. You will learn to see God's joy as an essential tool, as a gift, and as a permanent fixture that He wants each of us to have as part of our equipment here on this earth.

I believe that you will experience what I experienced as I read this book. It was as if Jesus was gently but strongly lifting up my chin so that I could look upward toward Him and His love and blessings for the purpose of bringing me into His *greater joy*! As a pastor, I see the need for believers to know how to access and release the joy of the Lord in their lives. There is a way to live in God's *joy*! Charlene shows us that wonderful way intended.

The message of this book is liberating and empowering. Because it is so solidly based upon scripture—the living Word of God—it stands as an authoritative prescription and roadmap out of the land of despair, fear, depression, and sadness and into the bright land of Jesus' *joy*—a place of victory!

Rev. Christopher Caton

Pastor—Word of Life Family Church

Preface

Have you ever considered smiling to be an art? How each person's facial features change slightly as they smile: some with dimples, some without, some with smile lines, some without, sometimes teeth and sometimes not, brighter eyes, and pinchable cheeks. Some of these physical features are more noticeable once the Botox wears off, and that is perfectly fine. The idea is that the smile changes from person to person, and no one smile is the same. This is what makes it an art. It is unique! The smile works our facial muscles and contours our facial structures unambiguously. Each of us has our own unique smile. Even when we are showing the duck lips, our smiles are still authentic to us. The smile is distinguishable from person to person. You know what else makes it an art? It is our specific creation. Yes, we create our own smiles, and we have the ability to share that creation with others. We choose to smile, and we choose to share it or not. A smile can be soft and gentle or forced and dry. Done out of sincerity or frivolity. We do it to be kind, cordial, respectful, to reciprocate, and in humor. The smile is our facial art, the encouragement we can share with others, an affirmation of something good. It is cathartic and curative, soul-driven and spirit-filled, undoubtedly infectious. As I think about the smile, it reminds me of the song by Louis Armstrong, "When You're Smiling." The lyrics of the song ring true for me. As I smile, I find that others tend to smile with me. Could that be true for you as well? Notice it next time you smile if the smile is returned or others are smiling with you. Perhaps the antidote to a frown or changing someone's world from upside down to right-side up is a smile. The smile, like art, is subjective and can be interpreted in numerous ways. A gaping, playful smile is my personal favorite to see in pictures with family. Think about your favorite smile. Where were you? Who was with you? What was happening?

When we sow a smile, we will reap a smile; it is the law of reciprocity. Luke 6:38 (KJV) reminds us to give, and it shall be given unto us with good measure, pressed down, shaken together, and running over the measure we mete shall be measured to us again. Sowing a smile is the least of the ways to give to others; hugs are a distant second. It might be acceptable for some and not for others based on the current climate. However, the good news is that a smile can represent a hug and involves no physical contact. We can flash a smile to a stranger and change their day. Maybe that smile will come when we least expect it or when we most need it, yet we can anticipate it will return to us. That smile can bring so much joy. When we cannot find our heavenly joy, the Holy Spirit can help us smile as a way to transport joy to us. I invite you to try it now. While thinking about a mildly frustrating or stressing event, take a moment to smile through it. That smile might be forced initially, but as you continue doing it, that smile can become more natural. Smiling through the pain, hurt, tears, frustration, and stress can be tough. I am not suggesting this is easy, having practiced it myself. I know it can be challenging for some people, but maintain a tenacious attitude. I may need a catalyst to help me smile. I reach down within my heart to identify what could be the source of a smile. Find some reason to smile through all the tough stuff life carries with it. Do it because you love yourself. You are worth it. Because of your family, children, or spouse, smile because it makes a world of difference between accepting heavenly joy and being one second away from sadness. Smile because you are creating art on your face, and you can share that art with someone else.

A smile typically reflects joy and excitement. We can find our heavenly joy sometimes through a smile. When struggling to find our genuine smile, it might help to grit our teeth and smile anyway. I am sure we have all done this at one point or another. When we aren't necessarily feeling like doing something, we do it anyway. Smiling is certainly more attractive than frowning and can brighten the mood. Like a budding plant or flower, we may have to go through various stages before reaching full evolution. The first stage of planting a flower is acquiring the seed and putting it in fertile ground. We are like flowers. As we share a smile, we are planting seeds. During the germination phase, the stem begins to push through the soil with the use of water, sunlight, and other nutrient-dependent microorganisms. Our smile might need to germinate over time with the help of external agents, such as a funny joke or someone tickling us, if internal factors do not bring us joy. We, like flowers, undergo photosynthesis in a different way as we get to produce our own smiles exclusive to us like plants and flowers produce their own food. Flowers bud during the reproduction stage, and at the stem of the flower, there are what look like little green leaves that aid in the sexual reproductive process. The petals of the flower are often very noticeable, brightly colored, and strongly scented in order to attract pollinators. Our smiles tend to be photostatic and sometimes a replica of a previous smile when involuntary. Though we may be constantly producing various smiles for different situations and settings, that smile attracts and captivates others. In the pollination process, flowers that are uni-sexed are counting on the wind, animals, rain, etcetera to carry pollen from one gendered flower to the next opposite-sexed flower for the fertilization process to happen. We pollinate our smiles as they become infectious, as noted previously, and are carried from one person to the next. We become impregnated with another smile as someone smiles at us—a smile is pollination in action.

Our smiles are God-given creative art that contains so much more than we think. We are like flowers, with our smiles reproducing and pollinating daily. It's a gift wrapped in a bow for some and a way to express contentment for others. It's also a way to convey gratitude, and though it has various meanings to so many, it is strength-producing and faith-engaging. The smile is a weapon against the enemy when under attack. You can put him in his place with a big smile and a hardy laugh. He will not get the best of you when you smile through the pain. The Bible has a myriad of scriptures regarding smiling and even outlines the benefits to our spirit, soul, and body. It's the best source for us to reference as to why our smile is so important. "A glad heart makes a happy face; a broken heart crushes the spirit. A wise person is hungry for knowledge, while the fool feeds on trash. For the despondent, every day brings trouble; for the happy heart, life is a continual feast" (Proverbs 15:13–15, NLT). I interpret this scripture as saying, "As my heart is glad, my face will smile." A happy face refers to a smile. A despondent person finds trouble in everything. And for those with a happy heart, every day is filled with gladness and a continual feast of joy. Learn to identify your smile in whatever you are experiencing. It might seem like an insurmountable situation, but be encouraged that you can get through it if you choose not to be despondent. Find a reason to smile.

Acknowledgments

I would like to acknowledge the God and Father of my life for the seed He's given me to sow into others' lives and hearts. I would like to also extend my gratitude to Pastor Chris Caton, my pastor, for the material he designed (The Love Test/The Thinking Test) for members of our church and gave permission for me to use. I would equally like to thank Pastor Christen Caton for the contributions she's made to my life as a member of WOLFC. To the team of professionals, editorial staff, and publishing team who helped get this book to the public, sincere thanks to you all.

Introduction

When I think about the art of my smile, I have a tough time being able to consider it art. First, I never really found my smile until I was in my mid-twenties, at the culmination of many hours and years of dental work. I know I am not alone. I am sure many folks can relate to having had dental work done. Previously, I wore dental brackets for a good three and a half years. The day they were removed, I was so elated, but prior to that, there was other work done, so it was quite the process. At the conclusion of it all, I found myself excited but equally experiencing some trepidation. I had not really smiled in years showing my teeth, so I felt so unprepared and not even sure how to smile showing teeth. It was emotionally awkward, I have to admit, but I had to stand in the mirror to rehearse smiling. I know it's a little lame, but it was sentimental to me because I never liked my smile. I guess practicing made me feel better, like I was going to improve it somehow. It was a clandestine practice I carried out for a couple of months after all the dental work was done. Sometimes, I am still keenly aware of ensuring my smile is correct. However, there is no correct way to smile and no rules that govern our smile. We are not bound by smiling with teeth, without teeth, or having crooked teeth. Yes, I know we place a lot of value on having a nice smile, but the key to making it art is the contrast, variety, composition, pigmentation, and patterns—our smiles do not have to be the same. Unfortunately, I learned that a little late, or I likely would have smiled more years before getting my mouth and teeth repaired. Art is subjective, and so are smiles. The beauty is in the form, harmony, texture, shape, and colors of each smile. We are craftsmen, masters, shapers of the art we create through our smiles. The smile entertains, inspires, is imaginative, and sometimes is inexplicable. I have certainly had those moments of smiling or chuckling to myself about something that may be antithetical to the situation at hand. I have learned that my smile characterizes me, and I do it more based on internal joy rather than external drive. Now, I smile for me, whether crooked, with teeth showing or without. If levity is present, immediately the smile is forming, and I no longer worry about the appearance of it. I just enjoy it. I think it's less important to worry about the opinions of others when we smile, as the Bible indicates in Proverbs 29:25 (MSG), "The fear of human opinion disables; trusting in God protects you from that." Human opinion should never get in the way of your smile as it did mine because that was disabling for me, but trust God because it will insulate you from the fear of public opinion. Smile because you want to or will yourself to do so because it's cathartic and mood-changing.

When we smile, we illuminate our heavenly joy, an illustration of the joy God has ordained us to receive. That joy is a gift from God, and we may not always sense it with our natural five senses. However, it is there in our spiritual awareness. We have to be more cognizant of it and spiritually attuned to it so that even when we do not sense joy and want to smile, we do it anyway. There are so many reasons not to smile and very few reasons to actually produce facial art, the smile. One of the biggest reasons to smile is that our heavenly Father loves us all, and whether we cling to the faith or not, He loves us. He loves you! Oftentimes, the devil, the enemy of our soul, does not want us to know this, and so he attempts to confuse us through our thoughts, interpretation of our visions, symbolic gestures, and even using people. We have to know that God loves us and discern correctly when the devil is trying to confuse us. The truth is found in the Word of God. He loves us all in spite of ourselves. And our smile amid certain situations reminds God and the whole heavenly host that we trust an Almighty God. We can bring acquittal to negative gesticulations from the devil with a smile. It is the opposite of what is expected when going through stressful situations, which should be recognized as the devil's tactics to confuse us. We can always smile when we know where and how to find our heavenly joy. In the chapters to come, we will review further ways to find our joy and smile. Conversely, we will look at some life situations that could be stealing our joy. Many scriptures will be reviewed throughout this journey as I believe the Bible is the source and road map for this lifetime. In Matthew 10:5–14 (KJV), Jesus chooses the twelve disciples and then sends them out among the Gentiles to preach, "The kingdom of heaven is at hand." The disciples were to "heal the sick, cleanse the lepers, raise the dead, cast out devils: freely ye have received, freely give." The disciples had received so much that now they were commissioned to give back. I am making an immeasurable hypothesis in the aforesaid scripture; however, I am postulating that the disciples were not walking around with frowns on their faces while doing these miracle-working assignments. I would like to believe they were smiling, particularly when they witnessed the power of God at work: healing the sick, cleansing lepers, and raising the dead. In verses 9 and 10, Jesus also tells the twelve not to bring anything with them, which is clearly an indication that they would be provided for by God. Now, there is a reason to smile as they trusted God to provide...and He did! In verse 14, Jesus provides encouragement, "And whosoever shall not receive you, nor hear your words, when ye depart out of that house or city, shake off the dust of your feet." Two points here to be made: We are the disciples Jesus chose *now* in this world, and He has also sent us among the Gentiles to do like the twelve disciples did *then*. We are protected and fully equipped to do what Jesus licensed the twelve disciples to do. We have to recognize the power and authority we have been given as Christian believers. As a result, we should be smiling, demonstrating our heavenly joy to our Father. Moreover, if we are not well received as apostles of Christ, we have to "shake off the dust," not give up, and keep going. Shaking the dust off will help us find the path back to being joyful and smiling. Jesus never told them to get upset and frown, start arguments, gossip about people, or hold grudges. He commanded them to "shake off the dust." I encourage you all to shake off the dust. We certainly cannot find our heavenly joy holding onto resentments and grievances. There are likely plenty more to come in this fallen world of sin, political pandemonium, and subversion. We have to rise above these evils and human iniquities to create art through our smiles. In verse 16, Jesus tells His disciples He has sent them forth as sheep in the midst of wolves, so they need to be wise as serpents and harmless like doves. We need godly wisdom to live in this fallen world among the wolves, but know that if we can endure to the end, we can be saved. Endurance can come through the hope that Jesus is returning and we will not be amid the wolves forever. Make the devil mad with your smile, particularly if you are going through something strenuous and burdensome. You are a formidable opponent against the enemy when you remain joyful.

As noted previously, it does not matter what your smile looks like or what is going on around you. The smile is art-producing and joy-affirming. All smiles are expected to be different, and it is a non-verbal part of our communication among each other. It is actually the rhetoric most commonly used to communicate with one another. Environmental factors, stressors, and even our attitude should not change the joy that we have to share. Being able to cast a smile in the direction of someone unexpectedly is truly a bonus of our faith and a blessing to the life of someone who needs it. There are specific rudimentary points that will be discussed as a way to understand and identify our heavenly joy. We will review several factors that can impact our joy, erasing our smile and subsequently robbing us of the ability to create facial art. Conversely, we will review nine biblical principles on how to find our joy. There are so many reasons holding us back from being joyful, and only a few ways to identify our God-given joy. We can't let dark clouds lingering in our lives steal our joy. Sometimes, we have to shout to shower in our joy and burst the cloudy moments. Demand your joy be released from the enemy's hands, and declare your joy cannot be stolen from you (Note: a declaration of joy will be provided toward the end of the book). The best way I know to do that is by smiling while going through the storm. Yes, we have the authority to do that should we choose. "For the joy of the Lord is your strength" (Nehemiah 8:10b, KJV). Declare it just as Ezra encouraged the Israelites to do. They went their way and made great mirth as they understood the declaration. Affirm this scripture with power and authority, understanding the gravity of your words. As we proclaim Jesus as Lord over our lives, we become royalty in the biblical sense. We are no longer ordinary people but extraordinary people by our faith in Jesus. We have the same strength, authority, and covenant as the Israelites, the prophets, and the disciples. We do have to recognize our royal apparel, the anointing of God, and put it on every day. Then, we can claim all things are ours, as noted in 1 Corinthians 3:21–22. Say it, "Joy is mine!" If you have lost your joy, it can be restored per Psalm 51:12. As David made this supplication to God, so can we. This is a great scripture to use in praying for joy for yourself. And this was not only a request for David, but he makes it on behalf of rabbles, those who rebel against the faith, as noted in verse 13. Our smile shows our salvation through Christ as it represents our joy. Make it a priority to smile even when you are not feeling like doing so. That could just be the beginning to restoring your joy. We have to cleanse our spirit and soul daily in an effort to maintain our joy. As we renew our minds in the Word, it will anchor us back to God's word but also wash us from all the junk that happens to us daily. Romans 12:2 actually makes an appeal for us to renew our minds daily, which will be an important piece for us to discuss. We will also dissect the difference between joy and happiness as they are sometimes used synonymously, but they are absolutely not the same. We cannot be deceived by what we are truly desiring—it is heavenly joy, not simply happiness, largely based on external components. Smile. You can do it regardless of what your smile looks like. Do it anyway. As you smile, it is gradually changing your attitude, demeanor, and cognitive process. I am not ignoring any of the concerns that could disrupt our joy; however, I am challenging us, including myself, to make a decision to smile. Life is tough enough. At least we have the right to choose joy and share it with others...that is a blessing. It is our gift to share. Joy for the Christ follower can be defined as a spiritual response and an enviable delight despite our circumstances produced by the experience of God's favor and coupled with the condition by which we understand as well as have revelation of His matchless grace and faithfulness toward us regardless of our wrongdoing.

I understood that my joy came from God based on my Christian belief. After all, isn't our Christianity based on the gospel of Christ, and that is the good news? The gospel is good. Shouldn't that bring us joy? Is there joy in the good news, or is it only adversity and affliction, as Paul advertises in the New Testament? I'm a Christ follower and advocate, but shouldn't I be serious about the Word without the veneer of secular joy? But what is joy really? Does it come from my faith, or is it found in the actions and experiences of life? I wondered at times if God really cared about us living a joyful life. Why should He? Doesn't He have more important concerns to address? I suppose He does, but because He loves us beyond conditions and beyond our transgressions, He wants us to be cradled in the abundance of joy only given from above. The Bible emphasizes many moral messages, but joy seemed to take a backseat to many of the appetizing messages that I heard in church growing up. Most messages were about fire and brimstone, and thankfully, I can say God's message has transcended from just having fire insurance. It is accepted as a more practical part of our lives and our relationship between Him and ourselves. It's about our faith, godly wisdom, living an abundant life, being authentic in our relationship with God, and so on. Heavenly joy just allows us to live an abundant life and be authentically committed to the God who loves us more than we can ever know. We have a covenant with Him that is not just about living biblical virtuous laws but by being connected to Him through His Son as He demonstrated His love toward us. We now have the opportunity to partake of heavenly joy. Why? Because we have been redeemed from the curse of sin and death. It's through this unbreakable partnership, better said a godly covenant, that we are recipients of certain promises established in the Word of God, and one of those promises includes God's unspeakable joy. It is ours for the asking. The passageway to it is by declaration of and acceptance in our relationship with Christ Jesus and foiling ourselves in the anointed word of God. The afflictions of our fleshly desires and sins don't strip us from having joy; however, we do have to realize that joy is ultimately from our creator, and we are His creation to be devoted to Him. Not devotion to our flesh or this earth. That devotion provides a dividend of joy. Though the ingredients for this heavenly joy must be found in scripture since His Word contains everything we need to live a godly life. All of God's promises are "yes" and "Amen" per 2 Corinthians 1:20, not "maybe" with an addendum to beg. You see, whether we know it or not, we are benefactors of God's mercy and grace, having accepted Him or not. In the amalgamation of grace, mercy, godly hope, and faith, we can overcome this earthly suffering, although, in the presence of it, the goal is to manifest joy and joy that surpasses our meager understanding. Paul overcame affliction as he talks about this thorn in his flesh. The supposition is that the thorn in his flesh was actually Satan. In reality, this man was after him in the chapters proceeding, but nonetheless, Paul recognized the meaning of this situation.

This thorn was to keep him humble and not get to a place where he is exalting himself above God and his own spirit. Oftentimes, throughout scripture, we see that the responses of the victorious are opposing to what we would expect as mere mortals. But in Christ, we aren't mortals. We are new creations and to be cloaked with garments of victory. Joy expresses victory, and we should put it on every day and speak the language of joy like we put on our clothes for spiritual warfare. We put on the breastplate of righteousness per Ephesians 6. And we put on the new identity we have in Christ, as Paul references in Colossians 3:12–14 (AMP).

> *"So, as God's own chosen people, who are holy [set apart, sanctified for His purpose] and well-beloved [by God Himself], put on a heart of compassion, kindness, humility, gentleness, and patience [which has the power to endure whatever injustice or unpleasantness comes, with good temper]; bearing graciously with one another, and willingly forgiving each other if one has a cause for complaint against another; just as the Lord has forgiven you, so should you forgive. Beyond all these things put on and wrap yourselves in [unselfish] love, which is the perfect bond of unity [for everything is bound together in agreement when each one seeks the best for others]."*

It's our spiritual clothing and new identity in Him. According to Galatians 5:22–23, we put on the fruit of the spirit, the result of God's presence within us, one of which is joy. We put on joy as it reflects the Christ in us to imitate the character of being a new creation. One of my therapy participants once asked me how I could put on joy. It's not tangible. It's not clothing like putting on a dress or a romper. Right was my reply: it's supernatural clothing we put on; however, I do believe there are elements to joy that can be tangible, such as adorning our face with a smile. Smiling with our eyes if sporting a mask. We put it on in our communication with monologues to ourselves in the mirror or in front of a camera and dialogues with others by the use of joyful vernacular.

We put it on in our decision-making with our temperament by deciding to be joyful. We put it on in our posture by standing tall, holding our head up high, straightening our shoulders, widening our chest, and remaining cheerful during adverse situations. We put it on as spiritual armor by maintaining joy in the face of despair and disappointment, laughing at the enemy, and praising God. We put it on both tangibly and intangibly every single day. We have to intangibly have a mindset of joy. Faced with this reality, she made the intentional decision to put it on like wearing shoes every day. She made it part of her daily routine as if putting on makeup or articles of clothing. She started her day in the bathroom mirror, reminding herself that she would maintain joy in the face of frustration today and asking the Holy Spirit to assist her by staying in the spirit. After all, it was promised to us and purchased at a high price. Scripturally, we will look at how we can put on joy, finding it through scripture and releasing it as an art. Joy summons the powerful spiritual forces of God to work on our behalf through whatever means necessary.

Table of Contents

Chapter 1

The Five-Point Tour

I want to make a couple of introductory foundational points before we can talk about finding and releasing our heavenly joy. If we can grasp these five points, it will assist us all in operating in our heavenly joy. The first principle point is that God is a good and a sovereign God. Jesus also referred to God as the only one who is good in Matthew 19:17 while speaking to the rich young man about how to have eternal life. Sovereignty means having dominion, supreme power, and authority. No other pagan gods can do what He does and have the omniscience and omnipotent authority He possesses (Psalm 103:19, Isaiah 45:5–7, 61:1, Jeremiah 18:4–6, Colossians 1:16, Ephesians 1:4–6). Not Dagon, Moloch, Baal, Asherah, nor any of the Egyptian, Babylonian, Roman, or Greek gods could do what the one true God was sovereign enough to do: provide us with a Savior. He is our authentic monarch, and heaven and earth are part of His monarchy. Secondly, Satan is real and working hard to steal our joy. What are we going to do about it? The enemy shows up in unforeseen and cunning ways. Do not trust him. His primary goal is to bankrupt you. The Bible refers to him as a thief in John 10:10 (KJV), and he only comes to steal, kill, and destroy. He will kidnap your joy and leave you desolate and defeated if you let him. The Bible warns us against his shrewdness, but we are to be wise as serpents and harmless as doves (Matthew 10:16). Thirdly, there are two forces at work in this world, both good and evil first noted in Genesis 2:17. The fall of Adam created this dichotomy and the sin nature of man. God has given us the right to choose between doing good or evil; both are set before us, and we have to make the ultimate decision (Deuteronomy 30:15). The present force of evil in this world is being restrained by the Holy Spirit until He gives way to the evil to come (2 Thessalonians 2:6–7). Fourth, man is not inherently good; otherwise, we would not need God. Our identity is rooted in Him from the beginning (Genesis 1:26). The fall of man in the garden is a significant reminder that we cannot conduct our life without Him. Adam and the woman were closest with God in the garden and were still overcome by the craftiness of evil. The best keepsake we can take from that experience is God's lack of faith in man to self-govern. We certainly need Him more today than ever. God the Father, Son, and Holy Spirit is our source to help us do good and make good decisions. We can find our joy in the goodness of God and the gift He gave us all through redemption of our sins by His Son (John 3:16–17). Finally, we are positioned here on earth, the stratus between both kingdoms of good and evil or heaven and hell. However, the good news is that we can have kingdom living here on earth. We can call forth whatever we need to do God's will on earth. God has made us authorized brokers to use the Word of God (Deuteronomy 30:14) to possess all that we need in this earth for those who are true believers of God (Proverbs 8:21, 28:10) and have accepted Jesus as Lord (Romans 10:9–10). Though that was not His original plan, the fall of man in the Garden of Eden was so significant that God had a better plan in mind that was greater or more glorious than the first (2 Corinthians 3:7–11, KJV). We become joint heirs with Christ Jesus, the second Adam, once we accept Him as Lord over our lives. This is the ultimate covenant God wanted to establish with us in that He sent His Son (part of Himself in the likeness of man) to be a propitiation for our sins to bring us back in right standing with Him (1 John 2:2, KJV). This covenant with God gives us the authority and power to possess kingdom living on earth. This should give us abundant joy that we are right with God, in covenant with Him, and because we are right with Him, then we can accept the grace gift through Jesus and be partakers of the covenant with God that affords us many blessings. I think we would all agree that joy is a covenant blessing. Let's examine these five points more closely.

God is sovereign even when we cannot understand His plans. He is benevolent and wants good for us, although sometimes He uses tests, which I will refer to as opportunities, in our lives to challenge change in us and stretch our faith. And also for us to view Him as almighty, for us to know we cannot accomplish anything in our own wisdom or might, and that we need to humbly trust Him. If we do not believe God's intentions are good for us, we will struggle with comprehending moments of opportunity and questioning God as to "Why me?" Additionally, how can you worship and love a God you don't believe is good to you and wants you to fail? In Jeremiah 29:11 (NIV), in a shrewd way, God shares a portion of His plan with us: "For I know the plans I have for you," declares the Lord, "plans to prosper you and not to harm you, plans to give you hope and a future." Every purpose that God has for us, whether it be identified by human knowledge as something good or not, we have to know God's intention is for good. Not to hurt us or to harm us. However, there are occasions when God will use something bad, sourced by Satan, to create good. For example, I once had a couple share with me that they were believing God to have a baby and prayed fervently for one of their own, so they didn't understand why God chose to take their baby away after he was born. I explained that God didn't take their baby away. It was definitely an act of the enemy, but He is using this situation to have you turn your back on God because He knows how emotional and hurtful it has been for you. They remained quiet and wept, as did I, because my heart could feel their pain. I reminded them not to let the enemy steal their relationship with God through this transfer. The devil's goal is to push them as far away from the kingdom of light as he possibly can. I encouraged them to move closer in their walk with God instead of jumping ship. Instead of praying for another child, pray that God works on their heart to remove the anger and bitterness so they can have joy for Him again. God was using this hurt to draw them closer, not to repel them from Him. Whenever they felt the anger and bitterness come up, they prayed Psalm 73:28 and personalized it. They found scriptures to add on to the initial one. As they began praying more and devoting more of their time to the church, hosting a life group and starting groups to augment the children's ministry, such as peer mediation groups they could use at school, God did bless them with a child of their own, a short year and a half after the physical death of their first child. God took what the enemy meant for evil to use for their good, and by donating more of their time to ministry efforts, God was able to transform their pain, which was the transfer in this transaction. Good for evil. Another good example can be found in scripture. We see that even with the Israelites, their release from Egyptian rule and slavery came from ten plagues performed by Aaron and declared by Moses through an act of God as power is given to him by God in Exodus 4:1–17. They had suffered greatly in Egypt, being enslaved for almost 400 years. Then, at the ninth hour, Pharaoh was regretting his decision to let them go because they were free labor to help build his city. However, he could not stand in the way of God's plans for his people. God knew the plans he had for His chosen people: to prosper them and not harm them, to give them hope and a future. We have to believe what the Bible says in Jeremiah 29:11 and allow that scripture to marinate in our hearts. All His intentions are good. We cannot always interpret God's plans or what He is doing, and that also makes Him sovereign. Romans 8:28 (KJV) confirms the following message: "And we know that all things work together for the good to them that love God, to them who are called according to his purpose." This tells me that He is allowing both the good and the bad to work together for His good and, in essence, our good; however, two components are necessary for that to happen: 1) a fervent love for God and 2) our actions are benefiting God's purpose. Since God judges and knows the heart (1 Samuel 16:7b), He will not be deceived by our outward profession of humility and Christianity but by inward works of evil and hypocrisy. God is the judge, and that is also what makes Him sovereign. In Psalm 50, God talks about being the judge specifically in verse 6 (KJV): "And the heavens shall declare his righteousness for God is judge himself. Selah." He is the judge in the earth according to Psalm 58:11 (KJV). We can read about God's judgment and benedictions over Israel throughout Exodus after their departure from Egypt. We can see God's sovereignty in both consequence and cursing, also in reward and blessing, as His commandments are followed. Even in consequence, God is good as He is looking to bring the hearts of the people back to Him. He wants to have absolute reign in our lives and for us to worship Him above all other gods. He shows Himself as the Almighty God ruling over all.

God's sovereignty is demonstrated in various ways in the Bible. For example, His many monikers are a part of His sovereignty. It characterizes His authority dissimilarly from all the atheistic gods of that time period. God created the whole earth and everything in it. He is God the creator Elohim in Genesis 1:1 (KJV), "In the beginning God created the heaven and the earth." God is also documented as God Almighty—El Shaddai in Exodus 6:3 (KJV), "And I appeared unto Abraham, unto Isaac, and unto Jacob, by the name of God Almighty, but by my name JEHOVAH was I not known to them." Moses is speaking to God, who is reassuring him that the Israelites will be redeemed from Egyptian servitude. Even in the use of the term Jehovah, God has many meanings. For example, *Jehovah Shalom* means the "God of peace," and *Jehovah Jireh* "the Lord will provide." He is Yahweh, first mentioned by Abraham when he is offering up his son as a burnt sacrifice to the Lord, and God supplies him with a ram in place of his son (Genesis 22:14). *Jehovah Rapha* means "the Lord who heals" and appears in scripture for the first time in Exodus 15:26 as God reminds the Israelites He will not afflict them with the same diseases as He did the Egyptians if they follow His commandments as He is the Lord who heals. *Jehovah Nissi*, "the Lord is my banner," is introduced in Exodus 17:13–16 when Moses offers up this designation after building an altar in celebration of the defeat against the Amalekites. God refers to Himself as the "I AM" in Exodus 3:14 (KJV). Moses is again having a conversation with God about the declaration God placed upon Him to go to the people of Israel, being held captive as slaves by Pharaoh, the Egyptians' monarch. Moses is questioning who he should say sent him. God responds in verse 14 with, "And God said unto Moses I AM THAT I AM and he said, Thus shalt thy say unto the children of Israel, I AM hath sent me unto you." The "I AM" phrase in Hebrew is accredited to Jehovah, as in the God who is the foundation of all existence. In Daniel 2:19, He is referred to as the God of heaven. In Daniel 4:37, He is known as the King of Heaven, all of which was used to distinguish our God from the Babylonian pagan gods that were worshiped during that time. He is also know as Emmanuel in Matthew 1:23 (KJV), which is interpreted as "God with us." Throughout the Bible, God has many epithets and takes on many forms, also reflective of His sovereignty. He is God Himself, God in the form of His Son Jesus, and God the Holy Spirit. Jesus the Messiah is prophesied about in the Old Testament but comes in the form of flesh as the Son of God in the New Testament. His birth is chronicled in Matthew 1:18–25. The Holy Spirit is noted as being the Comforter (John

26:7, KJV), who comes following Jesus' crucifixion to ensure us that we are not alone. In many forms and with many descriptors, God our heavenly Father demonstrates His influence and sovereignty. Even the enemy knows God exists and understands His sovereignty. The enemy must bow to Him. Do not be naive. We have to recognize the sovereignty of God in all His power and authority over creation.

God is a leader and all-powerful; however, He does use man to establish His plans. The beauty of it all is that whether we cooperate or not, His plan will come to fruition. The fall of Adam in the Garden of Eden did not withdraw our volition. God still gave man autonomy and dominion to govern and rule over his own person and in the earth, as noted in Genesis 1:28, Psalm 115:16, and Matthew 16:19. God would like for us to submit to His will; however, if we choose not to He will still be exalted and this is what makes Him sovereign. We cannot explain what God is doing or understand it at times. The appeal is that we are not expected to understand what He is doing all the time. His knowledge is above ours, and what He is doing is in our best interest. Isaiah 55:8–11 (KJV) speaks best to God's authority and sovereignty:

> *"For my thoughts are not your thoughts, neither are your ways my ways, saith the Lord. For as the heavens are higher than the earth, so are my ways higher than your ways, and my thoughts than your thoughts. For as the rain cometh down, and the snow from heaven, and returneth not thither, but watereth the earth, and maketh it bring forth and bud, that is may give seed to the sower, and bread to the eater: So shall my word be that goeth forth out of my mouth: it shall not return unto me void but it shall accomplish that which I please, and it shall prosper in the thing whereunto I sent it."*

God does not think like us, nor does He behave in a way that is comprehensible. But whatever His Word is set to accomplish, it will come to fruition. He is going to have His way in a manner that still respects our free will. For example, we might be praying for one thing and expecting God to show up the way we want; however, He might manifest His virtue in a completely different way. This very thing happened to Habakkuk as he was praying for his beloved city of Judah to be saved from the Chaldeans, and God showed up in a completely different way. In Samuel Whitefield's book, *Have You Been Blinded*, he references the story of Habakkuk in more detail as he notes the erroneous assumptions Habakkuk made about what God was going to do in Judah. He further explains that assumptions are shaped by our culture, human wisdom, our influences, our experiences, and our interpretation of the Bible. Yet we have to understand God has not abdicated His authority on this earth or in any nation and will not lower Himself to our assumptions. He will not be bribed by tears, money, or our devoted love for Him. He remained the sovereign king, even when He established kings and kingdoms as He holds the power to remove them also (Daniel 2:21). God answered Habakkuk, just not in the way he expected. The same is true in the story of Jonah, as God actually calls him to speak to the city of Nineveh to change their ways. He chooses not to go and flees to Tarshish. He felt the city was not worthy to be saved based on their wickedness, but God had other plans. He is reluctantly tossed overboard during a storm, swallowed by a great fish, and spends three days and nights in its belly before finally being spewed out on dry land as he decides to obey God. Out of his affliction, he cries out to God and is delivered from the belly of the fish. However, when God saves the city because of their obedience, Jonah prays to God in anger. God demonstrates to Jonah His sovereignty, illustrated by growing a gourd to protect him from the sun and then allowing a worm to eat it. Then, an east wind beat upon his head, and he fainted. Jonah shows such empathy for the gourd but doesn't demonstrate that same empathy for the people of Nineveh. God explains why He spared them, though He was not obligated. Nineveh is later destroyed by God as prophesied about in Nahum 2:1–13 and Zephaniah 2:13. God is *amazing* and will not be boxed in, outdone, stifled, or eradicated. We are not designed to be sovereign or to do things without God. We need the sovereignty of God as Adam did in the Garden of Eden, and so do we in present-day life, particularly in finding our heavenly joy. Our joy is further established by recognizing that God is sovereign and His desires will prevail.

Whether favorable or unfavorable things are happening all around us, we can have joy in that His plans for us are for good.

The second point is that Satan is real and working astutely and ambitiously to steal our joy. For those who do not believe Satan is real, I would challenge you to look at what is going on in the world now. I am not making this about politics; however, there are many evil things going on: mass shootings, plagues, nation against nation, and so forth. This demonstrates the evil that exists on this earth. Some force is behind that evil other than man. It's Satan. He is the real enemy. Man is capable of being used by either force, God, and/or Satan. Just look at King Saul, who was faithful unto God at the beginning of his reign, and this is why Samuel anoints him king over Israel. However, he sins twice against God without sincere remorse, and God leaves him. Saul had a narcissistic attitude and was tormented by demons toward the end of his life. In short, Samuel is called by God to appoint another king, and King David, the same young man who later defeats Goliath, the Philistine giant, is identified. Saul is subsequently used by the devil as he becomes jealous, then pursues David and tries to kill him. The full story can be found in 1 Samuel, chapters 9–19. If you have a Saul on your back chasing you down, confront it as David ultimately did. Proclaim yourself as a David generation people, remain strong, and defeat whatever Goliath or Saul is put before you. The enemy is real and wants to hurt anyone who is chosen, favored, and willing to be used by God. He is not coming for those who are already part of his kingdom. He is working on those who choose to be God's elect and live the righteous life. He who is precious to God becomes most important to the enemy. Now, that is something to smile about. If the enemy is after you, you must be doing something right. David was precious and chosen by God through Samuel. David was protected, although Saul had purposed in his heart to kill him. That protection came from God through man in the form of Saul's children, Michal and Jonathan, helping David escape. In a turn of events, David takes refuge in the cave of Adullam (1 Samuel 22:1), where Saul enters to relieve himself, and David has a chance to execute him but instead pardons him with grace. Similar to David, we will also be protected by our heavenly Father as we walk with Him and disengage the enemy. Take joy in that, and not in a dismissive way, but that you are protected by your heavenly Father who cares for and adores you. Likewise, do not allow yourself to be used by Satan, and do not be intimidated by his devices. We are encouraged to know Satan's devices, as noted in 2 Corinthians 2:11 (KJV). We can discriminate between right and wrong, but when being used by the enemy, we might think that what is wrong is right instead of seeing the evil in it. Some people toggle between both forces, being used by God or the enemy depending upon the wind of doctrine in their lives at the time, influencing their thoughts and infiltrating their hearts. Paul warns us about being tossed about with every wind of doctrine in Ephesians 4:14 (AMP),

> *"So that we are no longer children [spiritually immature], tossed back and forth [like ships on a stormy sea] and carried about by every wind of [shifting] doctrine, by the cunning and trickery of [unscrupulous] men, by the deceitful scheming of people ready to do anything [for personal profit]."*

Don't be tricked or fooled. Satan is real, and he shows up in ways that are least expected by using people to come against you, through deceit, or creating confusion by causing you to forget who you are and whose you are. These experiences will happen and can conceive in us a spirit of anger, resentment, evil, and so forth that could lead to us thinking we are doing right when we are doing wrong. "There is a way which seemeth right unto a man, but the end thereof are the ways of death" (Proverbs 14:12, KJV). Knowing that God is good does not absolve you from the pain of each peckish experience; however, knowing Him, His love for you, and His intentions toward you will get you through these experiences with grace and possibly less bitterness and anger.

Let's take a pragmatic look at how the enemy might show up in your life. It is sad that some folks do not believe the devil exists; however, he likely has shown up in your life, whether in overt form or covert form. His tactics are oppressive, destructive, seductive, and coercive. The enemy is a real adversary but not a worthy opponent. I do not admire or trust the enemy as I would with my heavenly Father. I describe him not to give him credit but so that you are aware. He steals, kills, and destroys, as the Bible tells us. We might focus too much on him, which is not the genuine goal, as we need to focus more on God. The more we talk about what he's doing, the more we give him reverence and demonstrate him as a worthy opponent. His destructive and evil ways might be part of your testimony, but remember to always share the goodness that God is doing in your life, every day and in every way. The love and goodness of God should be the loudest and most joyful part of your testimony. Jesus referred to Satan as the "prince of this world" (John 12:31, NIV). We are expected to be the "salt of the earth" (Matthew 5:13–16, NIV), not the devil. The person struggling with substance abuse, financial hardships, as in your car keeps breaking down, or home needs constant repairs, psychological disorders such as depression and anxiety, family discord, sexual temptations, feeling discouraged, confused, constantly miserable, all of these could be spiritual attacks from the enemy. He creates situations to bring about distressing emotions, impulsive decisions, and irrational behaviors that are sometimes uncharacteristic of who we are and certainly not the potential of what God has created us to be salt and light on the earth. We do have some choice in the matter, though, not succumbing to the enemy's tactics and engaging in staunch spiritual warfare against him. It is important to note the devil's former identity, at one point being an angel referred to as Lucifer, the son of the morning (Isaiah 14:12, NIV). He was attractive, bedazzling, and perfect until he sinned and was cast out of heaven forever. His iniquity was pride, as he wanted to be like God. He can never return to heaven regardless of what he does, and so he wants to take as many people with him to the pit of hell as he possibly can because misery loves company. We can smile because we will go someplace he will never be allowed entry to nor ever have access to harm us. As these demonic situations come up, our best defense is to smile and rekindle our joy. Remind him he is the father of lies and has no authority or role in your life by praising and worshiping God, praying, and whatever else God has you to do while going through the storm. God should have a precedent-making role in your life in giving you hope, encouragement, and support. The storm won't last forever, and you are stronger than the enemy and likely stronger than you give yourself credit for. God has given us authority over the enemy and has empowered us as ambassadors of Christ Jesus to use that authority per Luke 10:19 (AMP),

> *"Listen carefully: I have given you authority [that you now possess] to tread on serpents and scorpions, and [the ability to exercise authority] over all the power of the enemy (Satan); and nothing will [in any way] harm you."*

This scripture certainly allows me to express art through my smile. It might be a fight to do it for some, but I certainly would encourage it as it lets the enemy know he has no hold over you and you will not be defeated, discouraged, or disrupted in your mission to glorify God.

The third point is that there are two forces at work in the world, both good and evil. We want to blame God for everything, but we have to understand the agencies at work, both benevolent and malevolent forces trying to influence our lives. The good and evil that happen on earth work through mankind but are puppeteered by good or evil forces unseen yet very much in existence. God created us to love and worship Him and to choose light and life. We have the ability to choose how we want to live our lives as God gave us free will (Galatians 5:13) and dominion over the earth (Genesis 1:26). We can choose to do good or choose to do evil, and that is primarily based on the one we choose to serve and worship. Are you serving the devil, who is known to be evil, or God, who is authentically good. Let's just examine the words alone: if you add a "d" to evil, you end up with "devil," but if you add an "o" to God, you get "good." In plain perception of the words, we can see how easy it would be to associate one word with God and the other with the devil. I have always looked at good and evil in this way, but for some, they may have to train their brain to see it from this perspective. God is good! His goodness is manifested in various ways, and sometimes, we may not understand or think that God is trying to take revenge on us. In an effort for God to have His way, there are times when He will demonstrate His authority and power in incomprehensible and enigmatic ways. This is His unconditional will at work. He created us in His image and after His likeness (Genesis 1:26); however, after the fall, mankind's heart became sinful, and since we have the sin nature, sometimes we do evil things; it's not all the devil. However, we can change that to return to the good nature that God intended for us to have and thus be influenced by benevolent forces as we identify with God as our creator and His Son as our Savior. Then, allow the Holy Spirit to come dwell in you to navigate through life's changes and challenges. God could have made us robotically worship Him at will; however, He wanted us to have the autonomy to choose Him—to choose life and the good that He represents. "O taste and see that the Lord is good: blessed is the man that trusteth in him" (Psalm 34:8, KJV). I interpret this scripture as saying we get to take a sample of God to see how good He is, and as we see the goodness in Him, we trust Him and become blessed. It might seem strange to think that we can sample God's goodness as if sampling an item from a charcuterie platter; however, this scripture lets us know we can. Take a sample of His goodness, test it for yourself, and choose the agent you want to serve. In Psalm 145:9 (KJV), it tells us, "The Lord is good to all: and his tender mercies are over all his works." God is good, and as we align ourselves with Him in covenant and trust Him, we also become good like Him. Even with our human nature, He still sees us as good, not that we are necessarily good in our own conduct, but that the Son of God, Jesus, in us helps us become good in God's eyes. By accepting Jesus, we become justified to the Father because of Jesus' goodness. Jesus understood God's goodness. In the story of the rich young ruler, He refers to Jesus as "Good Master," and Jesus explains to him there is none good except one, and that is God (Matthew 19:16–17, KJV). God is associated with being good, and if we are in the kingdom of God, we ought to do good as we represent Him. In Ephesians 5:1 (AMP), we are expected to imitate our heavenly Father, "Therefore become imitators of God [copy Him and follow His example], as well-beloved children [imitate their father]." We should ask ourselves if we are imitating God with our goodness towards each other. Being good should make your heart joyful. In the goodness of God, there is joy. The luster of our joy should emulate God and shine outside of us in our demeanor and on our face. "The Lord is good and a stronghold even in the time of trouble" per Nahum 1:7 (KJV). What good is the joy we have if it's not shared with others in a smile, a hearty laugh, or even tears of joy? I want my aptitude, actions, and attitude to mimic God's goodness. I want to hear the words, "Well done, My good and faithful servant," so that I can share in the joy of my master (Matthew 25:21; 23, AMP).

The first evil act committed besides the disobedience of Adam and the woman, later to be called Eve, upon their exit from the garden was that of their son, Cain, who committed the very first murder, fratricide, towards his brother, Abel. He was influenced by evil as he allowed himself to give in to malevolent emotions and thoughts. Both Cain and Abel were giving their first fruit offerings to God, and Abel's was accepted while Cain's was rejected. It had nothing to do with the sacrifice itself but how both "presented themselves" to God. The Bible shares that God confronts Cain about his anger. Genesis 4:6–7 (NLT),

> *""Why are you so angry?" the Lord asked Cain. "Why do you look so dejected? You will be accepted if you do what is right. But if you refuse to do what is right, then watch out! Sin is crouching at the door, eager to control you. But you must subdue it and be its master."""*

Clearly, Cain looked dejected as God addressed that with him—obviously reflected in his countenance. Essentially, God is telling Cain if he does the right thing, he will be accepted. There is a certain amount of joy that comes from doing what is right and a certain amount of distress that comes from doing what is wrong. God goes one step further in reprimanding him by saying if he does what is wrong, watch out; sin will be waiting. If you choose what is evil, sin is the natural next step. He has to conquer and power over sin, the evil that wants to overtake him. Unfortunately, Cain doesn't heed God's warning. One day, he asks his brother, Abel, into the field and slays him. While not indicated, it almost seems implied that Cain plotted his brother's death. Cain allowed his anger to kindle within him, resulting in an evil act against his brother, what today would be known as first-degree murder. He is later rebuked and damned by God. This is an act of vengeance for his brother's death and Cain's consequence. Cain allowed himself to be mastered by sin, and evil overtook him. Whenever we put ourselves in a position to be overtaken by sin, evil will always dominate. It's crouching at the door. We cannot afford for the enemy to win in these last days. The good of God has to prevail over the evil of the devil. We have to do what is right because, in this way, we will find and release our heavenly joy.

The story of David and Saul certainly mimics a tale of good and evil. Saul was both a man of wisdom and imprudence. The first king of Israel appointed by Samuel as they rejected God as their king (1 Samuel 8:7). The Bible described Saul as "a choice young man, and a goodly: and there was not among the children of Israel a goodlier person than he" (1 Samuel 9:2, KJV). He and his kingdom were blessed as he followed God's command; however, he fell ungraciously when he began putting other gods before the One True God. God gave him a commandment, and he chose not to follow the commandment. Anytime God gives a commandment and we choose not to follow it, we are putting other gods before our One True God and King. His first sin was at Gilgal when he offered a burnt offering in sacrifice to God, demonstrating his fear of the Philistines instead of waiting for Samuel, his spiritual guide, to offer the sacrifice. Samuel was favored by God, a prophet and spiritual leader of Israel. As the chosen of God and judge of Israel, it was his responsibility and divine right to make this sacrifice, not Saul's. His second sin is when he doesn't destroy all the possessions of the Amalekites and spares the king along with animals, which he tells Samuel he plans to use the animals as a sacrifice to the Lord. God became displeased with Saul for not genuinely repenting nor following his commandments yet again. He didn't do what was right, and thus, sin was crouching at the door, as indicated in the previous paragraph. That fall displaced Saul's position with God, allowing the devil to govern him and evil to rule in his heart. Saul, still enthroned, soon to be dethroned, becomes jealous of David, the new king called by God and appointed by Samuel. He chooses David based on a word from God, not of his own accord. David is planted in plain sight of his enemy. He was to overthrow Saul because of Saul's sins. Remember, Saul is a wise man, so he likely understood what was happening. That leads to Saul chasing David across foreign lands on the prowl to kill him. As previously mentioned, David was protected by God, and even members of Saul's family provided him protection. David spares Saul's life not once but twice, a manifestation of God's goodness in him. Saul is eventually pursued fervently by the Philistines, who kill his sons, and Saul concedes by falling on his sword, death by suicide, as his armorbearer refused to thrust his sword into Saul as he beckoned him to do. Saul, a man after God's own heart, becomes disobedient, falls from grace, and is overwhelmed by evil to the point of trying to kill his successor, David. Each king appointed over Israel does some wrong or evil in the sight of God, always warranting a successor to be king. Israel asked for a king, but the best and last king of them all was King Jesus, and per Acts 10:38, it talks about how Jesus went about doing good. That is the only guarantee of good in this kingdom here on earth, which is the good that comes from God in the form of Himself, His Son, and the Holy Spirit. That goodness is reflected in our behavior as we submit to Him.

Fourth point: man is not inherently good; otherwise, we would not need God. Our innate nature is sinful based on the fall of Adam in the Garden of Eden. Our God adopted us into His kingdom and made us in His image so that as we accept Christ Jesus as Lord of our lives, we can appreciate and live the God kind of life He has for us. None of us are marginalized in God's eyes; we have all fallen short of the glory of God, and He wants us all to be saved. Being in the perfect will of God and following His precepts should give way to inexplicable joy and happiness. We have to get back to the business of doing good, and that can be tough, especially in this tepid climate today, but the God-like nature can assist us with that. There are times when we may want to do the wrong thing, for example, not forgiving a friend or enacting our own recipe of revenge on someone who did us wrong...we all know it happens. We all have likely slipped and given into the evil we should not do. However, the Bible cautions and even challenges us in Romans 12:21 (KJV), "Be not overcome of evil, but overcome evil with good." Some may ask how God can expect us to be good all the time when some people are so bad toward us. Well, He definitely does expect it, but not in our own power, as He understands that we cannot do it on our own. That would be so unfair of our loving and just God to ask us to do that without equipping us with the tools needed to externalize this expectation. He is hoping that all will come to the knowledge that Jesus is their Lord and Savior, and by accepting Him as Lord of their life, they will not be alone in this Christian walk. You have spiritually stepped out of your sin nature and into God's grace and forgiveness of your past, present, and even future sins, as God knows them all. As you learn more about the God nature and the Holy Spirit, who is our Comforter and Guide, then you can live and lead a good life. We cannot do it on our own, but the Bible lets us know with God, all things are possible (Matthew 19:26, Mark 9:23, 10:27, 11:24, Luke 1:37, 18:27, and Philippians 4:13), which includes being good. Being good, doing good, and having a good attitude are needed ingredients for releasing your joy.

God's wrath falls on the sin nature of mankind in Genesis 6:5 (KJV), as He stated, "And God saw that the wickedness of man was great in the earth, and that every imagination, of the thoughts of his heart was only evil continually." This evil nature in mankind is what provoked the flood and destroyed the earth. Noah, God's elect, was chosen to be spared and came into covenant with God after the flood ends. This covenant with God kept him in right standing and virtuous in the eyes of God; thus, he continued to do good. However, this goodness did not last through all generations as the people again do evil in the eyes of God by rejecting His instruction to replenish the earth and decided to build a city and a tower whose top may reach unto heaven (Genesis 11:4, KJV). It's later called the Tower of Babel as God confuses the language of mankind in reproach of their idolatry. This is significant because, at one point, all the people spoke in one language and could understand each other to come together against the will of God. Their imaginings were evil, and by confusing the language, God arraigned their intent. I believe that is why language is so significant today—so that the imaginings of mankind cannot run away from God in its own self-destruction since there is power in us all being in one language and of one mind. In essence, God is trying to prevent us from self-sabotage. Throughout history, mankind continues to demonstrate their need for God even in the destruction of the beautiful twin cities; Sodom and Gomorrah is evidence of that fact. The people who inhabited these cities rejected God by doing their own thing and ignoring the law, thus leading to the destruction of these cities because of their sin. But Lot and his family were spared by God. We are not alone in our walk to do good and stay in covenant with God. In this next sacred text between Abraham and Abimelech, God's presence is tangibly witnessed in a dream to Abimelech as he learns that Sarah is not Abraham's sister but indeed his wife (Genesis 20:1–7). Abraham was dishonest about

Sarah being his wife. Abimelech could've fallen into sin had he not heeded the warning of God. Abraham was in covenant with God, and thus, he was protected and his wife restored to him. We can see even in this passage that God helped Abimelech remain righteous. We need God because we are not inherently good, and sometimes our imaginations run away with us, as in the days of Noah, or we are given into fleshly desires like Abimelech. We may have a desire to be good like Noah and the motivation to do what is right, like Abraham, but without God, we cannot accomplish these things. Possibly, in the beginning, we can do what is right in our own might, but as scripture has shown in time, we will fall without God on our side. I dare say there should be joy that comes with knowing God is on our side. He actually intervenes at times to protect His chosen, as He did with Lot and Abimelech. He can tangibly show Himself to us, as He did Abimelech, so that we refrain from sin, but only if we invite Him. Thanks be to God our Lord, who always wants and causes us to triumph (2 Corinthians 2:14).

The need for God in order for us to do good is deposited more into our spirit in John 14:26 as Jesus is telling His disciples that He is leaving to prepare a place for them in heaven, but they are not alone since the Holy Spirit will be with them. The Holy Spirit sent by the Father shall teach them and bring to their remembrance whatever is needed. That same Holy Spirit is present today, and we can pull on Him for whatever is needed so that we can do good and experience heavenly joy on earth. The problem with the church is that they do not call on the Holy Spirit enough. He is our best source for operating in the goodness of God and staying in heavenly joy. Our goodness is not because of us or our works; the good we do is because of the Holy Spirit through the trinity of God, who desires above all that we do good, that we yield to Him, and that we live a righteous life. Paul shared in our woes on trying to do good. "For I do not do the good I want to do, but the evil I do not want to do—this I keep on doing" (Romans 7:19, NIV). Paul goes on to explain that if he does evil, it's the sin that dwelleth in him that does it. When he wants to do good, evil is present (v. 21). Do you find that when you want to do good, evil abounds? How do you reconcile the evil that is present with the good that the spirit wants to do? Evil is present in the body, referred to by Paul as "his members," but our "inward man," the spirit, wants to do good (vv.

22–23). So you can understand Paul's dilemma as he is constantly waging war against the sin nature, the humanly innate side of us that at times wants to do evil and steals our joy. I am not necessarily talking about the evil of criminal acts but also the evil of unforgiveness, retaliation, staying in anger, or simply allowing the flesh to rule over your spirit. We might also be waging war against the sin nature that stubbornly wants to remain even after we give our lives to Christ and submit to his will. When we become saved, our spirit is revitalized in the Word of God, but our flesh does not get saved. The regeneration that happens at the point of our salvation and the justification that occurred by Christ Jesus is at the behest of our creator, but the sanctification of the body comes in time as we continue to dedicate our lives, thoughts, and bodies to God. So, the sin nature still remains and befuddles us with how to manage it after making that commitment to God. During our salvation, we become one with Him, and individually, each of us comes into covenant with our God, but that is more of a reason for the sin nature to abound, to drive us away from the good of God. This fight with good and evil is not easy. We have to engage it daily but know that God is with us. If we are under the grace covenant with Jesus, we no longer have to worry about being good in our own might because we know we have God! He is good, and we just have to continue saying yes to Him. Romans 6:6–7, 14 (AMP) states,

> *"We know that our old self [our human nature without the Holy Spirit] was nailed to the cross with Him, in order that our body of sin might be done away with, so that we would no longer be slaves to sin. For the person who has died [with Christ] has been freed from [the power of] sin. For sin will no longer be a master over you, since you are not under Law [as slaves], but under [unmerited] grace [as recipients of God's favor and mercy]."*

This is key for us to recognize in this scripture that we are under grace, and thus, we have the ability to do good because of the covenant we have with God. We do not have to be slaves to sin because our sins were nailed to the cross with Christ. However, our decisions will lead to actions that are either in fidelity with God's Word or not. Even though our sin was nailed to the cross, we still have free will in our decision-making, although we should not use that free will to make sinful decisions. And this is why we need God: because our faith in Him accesses His grace. The above scripture also indicates to me that sin has power, so when we give in to it by doing evil, we strengthen its concentration over us. But remember this point: we have mastery over sin and evil because our flesh died with Christ, and we have a renewed mind in Him. Essentially, we have adopted God's thoughts as our own; that is the renewed mind. We can rejoice because sin doesn't have dominion over us as Christ followers, because we are not alone in this walk to do good, and because we have been given grace through faith by Christ over our sins. The sin nature does not have power over us, but we must remain spiritually minded to live in the goodness of God rather than carnally minded, giving way to sin and death (Romans 8:6). The answer to the query above is in this resolution: to use the Holy Spirit in your daily life, to recognize that you are no longer under sin, but called to grace, and that sanctification occurs over time, yet you must choose to do good. Finally, remember that if you find yourself in a position of not doing good, God is able to cover our sins if we earnestly ask Him for forgiveness. We can have joy in the fact that there is atonement with God through our Lord Jesus (Romans 5:11).

The last foundational principle for operating in our joy is the understanding that though we are positioned here on earth, the stratus between both kingdoms of good and evil or heaven and hell, the good news is that we can have kingdom living here on earth. I am sure that is hard to believe for some, but the Bible elusively and directly makes mention of this, for example, in understanding that what we say on earth has power. We can bring to pass kingdom living here on earth as the Bible says, "a wholesome tongue is the tree of life" (Proverbs 15:4a, KJV). We have the tree of life in us, similar to the tree of life that came from the Garden of Eden. We have life forces in us to bring kingdom living here on earth. Earth is a kingdom of both good and evil; however, we can see the good we want by doing and speaking the good we want (Romans 4:17b). Our tongue is an important and strong member of the body to the point of bringing to fruition those things we say which is why the Bible admonishes us to take care in how we say things and what we say

(Job 9:20, 22:28, Psalm 34:13, Proverbs 18:21, Matthew 12:37, 15:11, and James 3:8–11). The aforesaid will be profound in understanding why we can have kingdom living here on earth, although this is not the final destination for those who are true believers and accepted Christ as Lord. In Matthew 16, Jesus is asking the disciples, "Who do men say I am?" Simon Peter goes on to answer His question accurately as Jesus points out that His heavenly Father must have told him. This is very important to interpret that we can have kingdom living here on earth through access to the Holy Spirit, who provides us with wisdom and revelation knowledge as He did with Peter. He told him how to answer Jesus. Jesus goes on to share in verse 19 (KJV), "And I will give unto thee the keys of the kingdom of heaven: and whatsoever thou shalt bind on earth shall be bound in heaven: and whatsoever thou shalt loose on earth shall be loosed in heaven." First, let me point out that Jesus specifies which kingdom we will have the keys to, indicative of there being more than one kingdom. If there were only one kingdom, there would be no reason to make it clear in this passage what kingdom keys we are to be blessed with. The second point is that Jesus explains we have the ability to bind and loose on earth, the kingdom in which we all dwell now, and we have the authority to bind and loose with our mouth. What we bind on earth by what we say will be bound in heaven, and thus, what we loose on earth by what we say will be loosed in heaven. We can bind and loose from one kingdom, earth, to the next, heaven, by what we speak. This is the mighty power we have to obtain kingdom living here on earth by binding and loosing with that unsavory member of the body that James identified as unruly in James 3:8, the tongue. However, as we remain in right standing with God through the confession of Jesus as Lord, and living our faith walk by renewing the mind daily, taking caution with what we expose ourselves to, then we can speak righteous words, words that honor God and invites kingdom living on earth. We are in this world, but not of this world, and in order to remember the difference, we have to challenge ourselves to engage in righteous living through church fellowship, praise, and worship, renewing the mind in the Word of God, prayer, fasting, Holy Communion and choosing to live a sinless, righteous life. These are ways to bring us back in line with our faith walk in God's Word. The world influences our thinking daily in subliminal ways, and the bombarding of such material can change our thinking and harden our heart to the point of speaking contrary to God's Word. As can certain harsh and hurtful experiences that have changed our conceptualization of God as being good. We have to ward off worldly influences and desires. We have to let go of the root of bitterness. "For the kingdom of God is not a matter of eating and drinking [what one likes], but of righteousness and peace and joy in the Holy Spirit" (Romans 14:17, AMP). This scripture details what can enable us to have kingdom living here on earth. It is not found in the things we like: eating, drinking, nice possessions. It is found in being in right standing with God, maintaining peace with each other, and claiming joy that can only be bestowed to us by the Holy Spirit. So through a righteous tongue, employing the Holy Spirit, along with peace and joy, we can have kingdom living in a place where both good and evil reside. The truth of our joy is known to the Christ follower and true believer that Jesus is coming again, and though we can claim kingdom living on earth, our kingdom is not of this world. Jesus made that clear in scripture as He said the kingdom of God is in you, so that's why we have kingdom living here on earth: because it's in us, not because it's found in this earth. Our final destination is where Christ reigns forever, and He will reign over the kingdoms of this earth (Revelations 11:15).

This world cannot offer us what God has promised us in His Word. However, God set us here for a purpose and did not want us to be plucked up just yet. The most amazing aspect of the kingdom of God is that it dwells within us for the Christ follower. The Bible makes that declaration in Luke 17:21. As Jesus is talking to the Pharisees about the kingdom of God, He explains, "Neither shall they say, Lo here! Or, lo there! For, behold, the kingdom of God is within you." So the kingdom of God is within us, and we are on this earth, so we have kingdom living here. It may not always seem like it, but bad things happening does not discount the kingdom of God dwelling within us. Are you taking it with you? Do you put it on like clothing every day? You don't have to feel it, but you must have confidence that the kingdom is in you and spiritually take it with you every day. We are between two kingdoms, but if we can conceive that the kingdom of God is ours to possess and to take with us each day, then hopefully, that brings some joy as we are here to do God's will. Having His kingdom in us daily creates palpable joy. The enemy cannot possess the kingdom of God. We have God-given authority and power in the kingdom of God to bind up Satan and all his minions and repossess our joy. It can be disheartening for some to think we are shipwrecked on earth, the place where both good and evil or light and darkness are intertwined. Despite that reality, God wanted us to be placed here as soldiers in Christ to bring back the lost souls to Him in hopes that we all will be saved. The plan is for us to continue Jesus and the original twelve disciples' work here on earth until Christ returns to rapture us up and eventually transform heaven within the earth. Ultimately, the job of the Christ follower is to manifest the kingdom of heaven on the kingdom of earth because it's within us. The good around us still has the support of the Spirit of God to create a kingdom living here on earth, but we can only do that by staying spiritually minded instead of carnally minded, which is hostile toward God, as noted in Romans 8:6–7 (AMP). Stay spiritually minded and let your spiritual mind lead you to God's joy in the kingdom of God. The best gift God gave us was to bring us His Son, Jesus, referred to as the image of the invisible God, the firstborn of every creature (Colossians 1:15), to redeem us from our sins and our faith in Him, in all three forms [God Himself, God the Son, God the Holy Spirit] should help us live a godly life here on earth. His wish is that all will be saved, but He cannot fulfill that on His own, and thus why we, the true believers, have been given that responsibility on earth. Our faith is not for us alone or to be selfish with it. Now that we have accepted Christ, the goal is to be ambassadors for Christ and help others come to know the God of all creation, of goodness, of justice, of joy, of hope, and of love. We are commissioned to do His will here on earth, and as disconcerting as that may seem to some, we will not be shipwrecked here forever. The kingdom to come will only be glorious and good, but for now, we must dwell together in as much harmony as we can muster and demonstrate light in the darkness, setting free those who are captive to sin and darkness and showing love as the great commission God has called us to. Yes, there is tribulation in this kingdom on earth, and Jesus talks about it in John 16:33 (KJV), "These things I have spoken unto you, that in me ye might have peace. In the world ye shall have tribulation: but be of good cheer; I have overcome the world." We will overcome the world, take security and peace in that, just as Jesus overcame the world, we will also. Jesus deprived the enemy of the right to hurt, destroy, or make us fail in this earth as His intercessory prayer on our behalf in John 17:14–15 (NIV) states,

> *"I have given them your word and the world has hated them, for they are not of the world any more than I am of the world. My prayer is not that you take them out of the world but that you protect them from the evil one."*

Jesus is praying for our protection in this world. I am beyond thankful and joyful for Jesus interceding on my behalf for my protection in this earthly kingdom as we all should. Sometimes, interaction with the worldly kingdom can create friction for the believer. But we reach a place of sanctification the more we draw closer to the things of God in the face of evil. We have to believe God is for us and wants us victorious. I smile, simply meditating on the scripture in John 16:33. Jesus understood that there is evil in this world as He makes that known in this scripture. However, although evil exists, we shouldn't be overcome by it but overcome it by speaking God's word, the word He put in us, and by doing good (Luke 6:27–31). Remember, the kingdom of God is within you! Jesus is endorsing us and giving us security to do all that God has called us to do. We have to be willing to accept the challenge God has called us to, are you?

We can all recognize that the kingdom on earth represents both the kingdom of light and the kingdom of darkness. We can see this in our everyday life: those who live according to the light, which reflects the goodness of God, and go about doing good on the earth. However, there are also those who walk in darkness, not knowing the light and thus engaging in carnal and corrupt behaviors. It is so obvious to us who are in the light to recognize the difference, but for those who are not in the light, the Bible says their eyes have been blinded (2 Corinthians 4:4). Let's focus a little bit more on sight because that is an important aspect to the kingdom of God just as much as what we say out of our mouth. Jesus is speaking to Nicodemus, one of the Pharisees and ruler of the Jews, as Nicodemus is trying to understand the power that Jesus possesses to do miracles, which he believes must be from

God. Jesus responded with this statement in John 3:3 (KJV), "Jesus answered and said unto him, Verily, verily, I say unto thee, Except a man be born again, he cannot see the kingdom of God." We cannot even visualize the kingdom of God, which is the kingdom of heaven, unless we are born again, as in giving our life to Christ. This means this kingdom only resides in those who are born again believers; that's how you see it with the spiritual eye. Without that visual, it is scarcely possible to live or walk in God's kingdom living here on earth. The first step to understanding the kingdom of God is to be born again so we can see it, and then we can know the kingdom is in us. If that's true that the kingdom is in us, then wherever we go, we bring the kingdom with us. We need to have sight of the kingdom that we are representing. The Bible makes a distinction between the two kingdoms and asks that we put the kingdom of God first. In Matthew 6:24–34, Jesus is speaking on the Beatitudes and warns that no man can serve two masters. We will either hate one or love the other. He goes on to talk about worldly desires and concerns, indicating that the Gentiles, the not-blessed and non-believers, seek after these things. In verse 33 (KJV), Jesus advocates for us to "But seek ye first the kingdom of God, and his righteousness; and all these things shall be added unto you." Jesus is denoting the difference in the kingdoms clearly requesting that we focus on God's kingdom, again delineating the different kingdoms that exist. He says that all things will be added and provided to us as we put the kingdom of God first. I am pretty certain that includes joy being added to us, even in this earthly kingdom. The flow of joy is a kingdom condition not to be reduced to a mental process. And so, we have to develop our joy from our spirit, not from the mental arena of our thoughts. We who walk according to God's Word are in the light and have been delivered from the power of darkness and have been translated into the kingdom of His dear Son. That is our inheritance (Colossians 1:12–13). Since both kingdoms of light and darkness exist on this earth, it is up to us to identify which kingdom we are choosing to align ourselves with. Jesus makes this distinction even clearer in John 18:36 (NIV). While responding to Pontus Pilate's question, Jesus answered, "My kingdom is not of this world. If it were, my servants would fight to prevent my arrest by the Jewish leaders. But now my kingdom is from another place." If we are partnered with Christ, then our kingdom is not of this world either. Make no mistake, anyone who identifies this earthly kingdom as theirs is not walking with God, and our perfect joy can only be found in Him (John 17:3). This world is depletable and will eventually come to an end. We have to choose the kingdom we will serve, and we cannot be of two minds about this choice. "If a kingdom is divided [split into factions and rebelling] against itself, that kingdom cannot stand. And if a house is divided against itself, that house cannot stand" (Mark 3:24–25, AMP). We cannot be divided in our decision regarding the kingdom we will serve. I would suggest choosing the kingdom that provides you with the most benefits in the end, not temporarily, but renewable benefits. We might be in this earthly kingdom for a time to serve God's purpose, but eventually, we will be plucked up like calves from a field. "For the Kingdom of God is not just a lot of talk; it is living by God's power" (1 Corinthians 4:20, NLT). First, choose the kingdom you will serve, and then live by it, not just in words alone but by living in the power, as in pregnant with God's authority, of His kingdom on earth.

These five foundational principles are necessary to understand before we can begin talking about finding and releasing our heavenly joy. The reality is we are approaching eschatological times, and in an effort to remain joyful and encouraged, we need to know and understand these points pursuant to what is about to happen. God has clearly shared these points throughout the Bible with us for a reason, as He wishes that none should perish. His word will remain the same throughout eternity, and that word found in the Bible is our road map for life. Isaiah 40:8 (AMP) states, "the grass withers, the flower fades, But the word of our God stands forever." Thankfully, His word will stand forever, and each of these foundational points can be identified in His Word as a way for us to navigate through this life. He knew that it wouldn't be easy for us, nor did He expect it to be. Remember, a servant is not greater than his master (Matthew 10:24). You may not want to smile at these principles, but I think it gives you reason to smile more and even brighter. God is sovereign. He is good. It is because He is good that sin and evil will be punished. Good will triumph over evil. He sent His Son, in the form of flesh, to redeem us of our sins and the evil we would do we do not as a result of the love Jesus has demonstrated toward us. And although Jesus is not physically present with us, we are not alone. We have the Holy Spirit to govern our actions and our tongue and to guide us on the righteous path. We can now live a righteous and good life because we are no longer under sin but under grace. We have to choose grace every single day. We have grace protection in spite of the evil that happens here on earth. Jesus defeated Satan, and so we are conquerors as we accept Him as Lord over our lives. He is also praying for us in heaven to be protected from the evil that would befall us or the temptations that would overtake us. Although bad things happen and temptations may come, do know that it could be for your good. Remember, God works all things together for our good. You can fight against evil with the Word of God as your sword, the art of your smile on your face, and allowing the Holy Spirit to provide you with the wisdom needed to overcome. Don't be beguiled by earthly and fleshly desires; it's not the way of righteousness and only leads to death. Smile because Jesus has given you resurrection life. Smile because Satan is under your feet. Smile because you are walking in the goodness of God. Smile because you can overcome evil with good. Smile because it's your active defense against the enemy. Smile because you can. Smile...smile...just smile, simply because God loves you.

Chapter 2

The Joy That Comes from Walking by Faith

As Christian believers and Christ followers, we are expected to walk by faith and not by sight. This passage can be found in 2 Corinthians 5:7 (AMP), "for we walk by faith, not by sight [living our lives in a manner consistent with our confident belief in God's promises]." I am supposing that if I were to live my life in a manner consistent with God's promises, I would be smiling with abundant joy. God's promises will not fail, and as aforementioned, His promises will come to fruition; however, we do have to walk by faith, the faith that comes from knowing, trusting, and accepting God. If we walk by sight, we can become discouraged and fearful, particularly in this world since both good and evil are present, but walking by faith gives us access to God. He is able to make all grace abound toward us, His favor is forever with us, and His joy is always accessible to us. When we don't see things happening as we expect or want, that is the best time to walk by faith because it's also the best time for the enemy to dissuade and depress us. His goal is to move us as far from God's word, sometimes in the most gradual way possible. He doesn't want us to access God's joy because, through joy, we find our spiritual destiny with faith and hope in God's word. The devil is fine with us going to church, hearing a word every now and again, jumping and running and praising God, as long as the joy of His word doesn't become embedded in our hearts. Joy provides us with hope and helps us feel empowered and encouraged. Joy is the incendiary and innate mechanism to ignite our faith walk with God. These are tools that the devil doesn't want us to have because they lead us in the way of faith and walking by God's word. The enemy is doing his job, and we have to ardently do our job in maintaining the faith and being ambassadors for Christ. Remember, God is a sovereign God. When we walk by faith, He is with us and exposes us to His brand of angelic spirituality, not our own. When we choose to live life from His perspective and brand of spirituality, we will experience a little heaven on earth daily. We think we have an understanding of this faith walk as though doing good makes us equivalent to being like God, but the reality is we cannot do it without the trinity of God the Father, His Son, and the Holy Spirit. Our works do not bring us into relationship with God (Ephesians 2:8–9). Our faith in Jesus and accepting Him as Lord of our lives brings us into relationship and covenant blessing with God. This is the true essence of our faith. Doing good is a byproduct of our faith walk with Him. Our spirit needs to be reserved for God's brand of faith, not half-hearted or lukewarm faith. Our heavenly joy is tethered to walking in the true faith of God since this world cannot offer us anything eternal. The Bible refers to the things of this world as temporal and fleeting (2 Corinthians 4:18). For our joy to remain and to be full, we have to walk by faith that is only found in the Word of God. The enemy cannot offer us anything except for death and destruction in this world. Even happiness is temporary, which Satan may try to disguise as joy, but if we walk by sight, we will only be experiencing happiness, but never the joy that God wants for us. Please recognize that the source of your joy is tied to the master of all joy, and with godly faith, we bring joy with us wherever we go. We aren't waiting for joy to show up. Faith reminds us that it is discernible even when we don't see it or feel it. Joy is not felt through our senses. It's birthed through our faith. Faith is how we transact spiritual business with heaven, so use your faith, the currency of heaven, to receive your joy.

There is no promise of a pain-free life. Sometimes, we can become so focused on our own pain that we lose sight of the joy of God. God was also pained by having to give up His only Son, but He saw the sacrifice was great because His love for us was greater. The heavens rejoiced when Jesus laid down His life for us to provide us with everlasting life and eternal joy. It's a gift from Him that we can only receive by faith. You see, faith and joy work in concert with each other and feed from the same source. The greater our faith, the more joy we experience, and the more joy we have, the more it ignites our faith. Faith is needed for joy to flow, especially when everything is erupting around you. Let Him dry your tears and wipe away your sadness. He can usher in joy like a breath of fresh wind if you let Him...if you hold on to your faith. We need confident God-like faith that what is promised in the Word, God will do (2 Corinthians 1:20). He promised us joy according to Psalm 126:5–6, Ecclesiastes 2:26, John 15:11, 16:24, 17:13, Romans 15:13, 1 Peter 4:13 and Jude 1:24. I know for some this might be hard to believe that God has promised us joy, but don't stay in disbelief as that is contrary to what His Word states. God brought us His Son not just as a ransom for our sins but also in an effort that we might have joy and that His joy for us might flood in us and complete us so that we hunger for His word. The message of His birth is of great joy to us all (Luke 2:10). Trusting and believing in Jesus can deliver us from sorrow and transfer to us His eternal joy. As we develop our faith, over time, we can perceive the joy of God as evident in our lives. We have to elevate our faith to the dimension where we are looking beyond the physical realm into the supernatural realm, where God has stored many blessings for us, and one of those blessings is joy. I encourage you to expand your faith beyond all aspects of your life that don't bring you joy: the stress at work, the tension in your marriage, the disagreements with friends, the environment you live in, the conflicts at church, the burdens with finances or health concerns to receive the measure of faith God has given to us all (Romans 12:3). Some folks may become distressed temporarily by various trials, but I say trust in God's word through these trials because they come to try your faith but through our faith God is protecting us by His power. However, the Bible tells us there is wonderful joy ahead even though we must endure trials. We will rejoice when our faith remains strong through trials as it shows our faith is genuine. For our salvation will be revealed by the return of our Lord, Jesus Christ, as stated by Apostle Paul in 1 Peter 1:3–8. The return of Jesus might be the one aspect of your life that brings you great joy. Hold onto that revelation knowledge that Jesus is returning someday soon. The trials and circumstances might test our faith, but it should not tear us away from the truth in God—He is sending His Son to return for us. And these trials are like a sifting process for those whose faith is genuine to receive inexpressible joy by the return of our Lord as our souls will be saved. We also become patrons with Christ as He suffered inexplicable and indescribable trials (1 Peter 4:13). If you have nothing else to hold onto that brings you joy, hold onto that word that Jesus is returning someday and, with His return, a wonderful joy will be procured to us who have genuinely fought a good fight and kept the faith.

What is faith? It's well defined in Hebrews 11:1 (AMP),

> *"Now faith is the assurance (title deed, confirmation) of things hoped for (divinely guaranteed), and the evidence of things not seen [the conviction of their reality – faith comprehends as fact what cannot be experienced by the physical senses]."*

Your faith brings into recognition the joy you may not physically be able to see or experience in the carnal mind. However, in the spirit, your joy is full. Faith is developed through our spirit, and by the Holy Spirit in us, we sustain joy. As we actively participate in our faith, which is from God, we are networking with the creator of our joy so it becomes replenished each day. Faith is needed for what cannot be perceived in the natural. It's not felt through our senses or understood through our intellect. It's through our faith that we connect to joy. It is the currency of heaven, and in exchange for our faith, we receive supernatural joy that is inconceivable even in a crisis. As the Word states, to be spiritually minded is life and peace. If you need peace, get out of the carnal and get spiritually minded, which comes by entertaining materials that are spiritual and monotheistic to the One True God. The devil is trying to separate the spiritual from what is godly and holy, but they were never meant to be separate. It is homogeneous. I have had many folks tell me in my practice they are spiritual but not religious. That is a lie from the enemy because, as the aforementioned scripture demonstrates, it's not separate. The Bible is a religious artifact, and the term "spiritual" or "spiritually minded" is found in countless verses throughout this vestige, which we are to conceive is only about yoga, worldly meditation, nature, and worldly things. I think not. We have to see it the same. As we stay in the spirit, we can experience peace and joy in our heart, mind, body, and soul. We can only stay in the spirit through faith, not in our flesh. That is likely what is hindering many people from experiencing God's heavenly joy because they are so focused on the "spiritual" aspects separate from the Bible. And how do we build our faith? It's through the Word of God. The flesh is in a constant war against the spirit (Galatians 5:17), and as the spirit prevails, we can walk in faith. The spirit prevails by meditating God's word over, above, and beyond what we see, hear, think, or feel. Romans 10:17 shares a little more about how faith works: by hearing and hearing by the word of God, or as many ministers have said, it's by hearing and hearing and hearing over and over again. As we put God's word on repeat in our hearts and mind, we will begin to believe it. Anything we hear over and over will almost inevitably be believed and likely become our reality and influence our thoughts. And so, while growing our faith, we do have to be cautious about what we are hearing, watching, and mentally rehearsing every day. "Whatever you plant in your subconscious mind and nourish with repetition and emotion will one day become reality" (Earl Nightingale). Maintaining and ruminating on a confident faith in God will bring to fruition the joy that He has promised us. It will influence your thoughts, and what you think affects how you feel. We can claim that unspeakable and incomprehensible joy that is found in the Word of God as we pray and believe by faith without doubt in the heart (Mark 11:23–24). You receive it or seize it in the spirit, and you shall have it in the spirit. Receiving and manifesting are not the same. You receive joy in your spirit, and eventually, that will manifest in the natural. Give your faith time to work and pull on the Word so that it comes from the root to produce fruit. The fruit of joy is ours as we claim it; receive it by faith, even if you don't feel it or see it by sight in the natural.

Our pure joy comes from God. It was a provision made for us and destined to us as an inheritance when we were grafted into the blessing of our salvation. We are born again through Christ Jesus, God's Son, and thus our joy is composed by Him. He created joy and gifted us with an abundance of it. It is a privilege of those who are believers and Christ followers. Smiling and laughing are behaviors fashioned by God for us to enjoy. It's our armor, a weapon, a defense mechanism for some, a coping strategy for others. All in all, it can be cathartic and mentally sound rest for us to engage in these practices of smiling, laughing, and merriment, which epitomizes our joy. We might need to smile and laugh through faith, but it will bring us to a place of joy. I can recall conducting many sessions when we laughed our way through it, and genuine laughter that replaced sadness with peace and joy. And many of my therapy participants have reported feeling the effects of a laughing session for days after. It's the chuckle that you have while making dinner, the smile that comes to your face while getting ready for bed, or the amusement after meditating on a good-humored event, such as what my participants have experienced during sessions. I admonish you not to allow your joy to be tied up in the doleful experiences of the past or any trauma you might have endured. Recollect, even if by faith, what has brought you joy and hold tightly to that feeling to let it bring you uncompromised peace and high-spirited mirth. Although bad things do happen, our faith in God can transpose the dejection of the past and the adversity of this world by which our hope becomes operative to receive grace for the promises of God, and that is an eternal joy. We can have joy if we hold onto our faith long enough. Our faith makes joy possible!

Chapter 3

The Joy That Comes from Godly Obedience

Obedience to God's holy word and His precepts will always lead to pious joy. Obedience can be defined as "a sphere of jurisdiction, compliance, conformity, subordination, discipline, or surrender to the one who holds authority or power over you" (Random House Webster College Dictionary, 1997). Obedience to God's word brings us peace, and peace will always lend itself to joy. Not only is God asking us to be obedient to His word, He also wants us to be obedient to whatever the Holy Spirit tells us to do. Isaiah 12:3 (KJV) states, "Therefore with joy shall ye draw water out of the wells of salvation." The water equals the anointed word of God. And with joy, we draw the anointed word out of our salvation that we have with God. In our obedience to being saved by our creator (verse 2), we can experience eternal joy. The NLT version of this same scripture says, "With joy you will drink deeply from the fountain of salvation." This leads me to believe the fountain of salvation has something good that comes from it that is joy-producing. God wants us all saved, and with that salvation comes righteousness, miracles, anointing, blessings, peace, and so forth. That also includes joy in obedience to Him, which is tied to our salvation. It's a gift from Him. There are benefits to being saved, and salvation requires obedience. Being out of the will of God is consistent with disobedience, and disobedience always forces the wrath of God. We can look throughout scripture to see the results of disobedience. The Israelites wandering around the desert is a prime example of disobedience, and how about the story of Jonah running from God's dictum and subsequently finding himself in the belly of a large fish? Although these events happened,

God is not a harsh God, though He will seek vengeance for disobedience or injustice when necessary. And as a Christ follower, we would want that as God did with Haman, the Agagite, who desired to kill all the Jews in the story of Esther, but he ends up being killed along with his male lineage because of Esther's obedience to her uncle Mordecai. He was looking to wipe out an entire civilization of people, the genealogy of God, which would've stopped the birth of Christianity. Obedience was necessary then because the devil was trying to hinder what God had planned, the nativity of Jesus. Or Saul, the persecutor of Christians, who God transformed through righteous judgment and he became Paul, the apostle of Christ. However, God is very loving, and with genuine repentance, He was willing to forgive, and He does to this day. Think about the story of David. God forgave him after he plotted a murder against Bathsheba's husband, Uriah, the Hittite. First Peter 1:14 (AMP) provides the following directive,

> *"[Live] as obedient children [of God]; do not be conformed to the evil desires which governed you in your ignorance [before you knew the requirements and transforming power of the good news regarding salvation]."*

This scripture indicates apart from salvation, we were all ignorant, yet with salvation, we have godly wisdom. So, we are no longer victims of ignorance, living a life of disobedience unless we choose. This scripture also reveals that salvation has requirements and transforming power. This is the same transforming power that came upon Saul. It also refers to salvation as the good news. It's not enough to identify as being saved; as mentioned, our salvation has requirements and transforming power. Once we have knowledge of the requirements of our salvation, and we're no longer in ignorance, then we are given the transforming power to change those things in our lives that do not meet the requirement of our godly salvation. If we live similarly to the world but call ourselves Christians, we are hypocrites, and hypocritical behavior will never lead to joy.

Joy is produced from our loving obedience to God through righteous hope. As we go through the transforming power of salvation, we learn that being obedient is not a result of avoiding consequence. It's because we love God that we surrender to Him, and as we fall in line with what He's asking, obedience and love give us access to joy. We can see in scripture that a loving obedience to God through our salvation always leads to something good happening. There was great expectation, righteous hope from following God's word. Deuteronomy 28:1–14 highlights the blessings (or benefits) that come from obedience. If we obey God's word, this is the expectation we should have as long as it is indeed God's word and not our own. Any decision we make or anything we do should always leave us with a somatic sensation of peace in our spirit. Anything aside from that might not be the will of God. God will never tell you to do anything contrary to His word despite what people might believe. He will never tempt you or influence you to sin. He will never come to you double-minded, with confusion and uncertainty. So, if ever this has happened, it's not godly. Sometimes, we make decisions or do things and say it's God when, indeed, He had nothing to do with it. We have to be careful not to blame God because that is likely the devil's tactic to move you away from God, out of His obedience, His will, His commandments. But whatever you do, God will never remove you from the love He has for you. Even when you turn your back in anger on Him, assuming He guided you down the wrong path, He still loves you. And the prayer of the Holy Spirit is that your spiritual eyes be opened to see what the devil is attempting to do. In contrast to God's blessings, in Deuteronomy 28:47–48, God indicates what to expect if we choose not to serve Him with joyfulness and gladness of heart. However, the New Testament brings the saving grace of Jesus, God's redemptive Son, so there is no longer fear and consequence associated with disobedience but joy and thanksgiving because we can be forgiven of our sins because of what Christ did for us. Remember, joy for the Christ follower can be defined as a spiritual response and an enviable delight despite our circumstances produced by the experience of God's favor and coupled with the condition by which we understand as well as have revelation of His matchless grace and faithfulness toward us regardless of our wrongdoing. Even in our disobedience, we can still have joy through the forgiveness of our sins by repenting of transgressions. That same joy Jesus had, He wants us to have it also. That's why He became the sacrificial lamb of our sins. He wants the same joy He had to be in us, and that joy makes us complete. But that joy that Jesus is talking about only comes from obedience to our salvation. Jesus had joy despite the persecution and the life sacrifice He would become. It was the joy that came from His obedience to the Father that brings us supernatural joy out of our obedience to God. We mimic Christ when we obey what God tells us to do and thus vicariously experience the same joy. Obedience pleases God, and the ultimate fruit of obedience is joy.

Interestingly enough, we are less likely to obey a God who we believe doesn't love us, forgives us, or is for us. And so the devil has his work cut out for him, trying to get us to disbelieve that God loves us, forgives us, and is for us. Or, more importantly, trying to persuade us that His promises don't apply to us through some fault of God's or our own. But the truth is once you choose salvation in Christ, all the promises belong to you as you work your way up to sanctification. The devil knows this, so he cunningly plots against you. As long as he keeps you from believing what is true in God's word, then he can keep you from the authentic joy that God gave His Son to provide for you. You can read the Bible ten times a day, but if you don't believe and receive what you read, then the truth of God's word never gets inside of you. It doesn't permeate your heart, the part of us that communes with God. You are hearing the word, but it's not doing anything for you. This is similar to what Jesus talked about in Mark 4:2–12, and I like it from the Amplified version as Jesus talked to the crowd about the parable of the sower. I am breaking it down but would encourage reading the full passage. In this passage of scripture, the seed (the truth of God's word) fell on four types of ground based on the topography of the ground that determines whether the seed would yield fruit. If seed falls on the road, it's eaten by birds. If it falls on rocks, it's scorched. If it falls among thorns, it becomes choked, but there is the seed that falls on good soil and produces fruit. The fruit of the seed you receive has to be a greater truth to you than what the devil is trying to get you to believe. Jesus goes on to provide an explanation when asked by His disciples for an interpretation of this parable. He refers to it as "the mystery of the kingdom of God." It has been given to you, those with a teachable heart, but those outside, the unbelievers, get everything in parables. Jesus proceeds to explain why this is because there are those who continually look but do not see and those who continually hear but do not understand that they might turn from rejecting the truth and be forgiven. The truth is you have to see but beyond natural sight and hear but beyond your physical ears, and until you do that, you will never receive the truth, so you become susceptible to the enemy and easily persuaded. The reality is you will never yield the fruit of joy until you receive the truth of God's word.

Chapter 4

Nine Ways to Finding Heavenly Joy

Finding one's joy is not necessarily about the search; it's less comparative than that. It's more about discovering the source of one's joy. Our heavenly joy is rooted and grounded in the Lord; it's seeded in God's word, and it's a promise from God that can be experienced in this earthly kingdom by faith. Though we are only sojourners here on earth, God does want us to have joy while we're here. Your joy will not be found in this book alone; however, by understanding, employment, and mastery of these nine practices, you can be elevated to a place of joy. Heavenly joy was predestined for us by God from the beginning; however, because of the fall of man and sin, the joy we should freely receive may require effort through staying allied to God's word, specifically during circumstances designed to steal your joy. We need ways to rediscover our heavenly joy during moments of being bogged down with the fear, stress, and doubts of life, as our joy can become suppressed. When our joy is identified in Christ, then no man can take it from us per John 16:22. The difference between earthly joy and heavenly joy is just that it's found in Christ, and no man can take it away, nor any circumstances or roadblocks. It's a condition of your faith in the Trinity. That type of joy is a blessing from the Lord, and the Bible lets us know in Proverbs 10:22 that the blessing of the Lord makes us rich without sorrow. There is no sorrow in heavenly joy. We aren't expected to toil for something that was promised to us in God's Word. We only need to believe it and accept it. In my discovery of smiling and finding joy, the Holy Spirit revealed to me nine scriptures on the inception and nature of my heavenly joy. Our joy is not found in earthly possessions, other people, or a life without problems—that doesn't exist, but perhaps in fairy tales. The storms of life are inevitable and very real, but the joys of life can only be established in our faith in God. If we understand the genesis of our joy, we will always know how to find it again, even in moments of deep distress or feeling overwhelmed with fear. The goal is to put these scriptures into practice as a way to find and release your heavenly joy. There is no chronological order to this layout; it is simply in the order as the Holy Spirit revealed it to me.

The first scripture can be found in Psalm 119:33–35 (KJV),

> *"Teach me, O Lord, the way of thy statutes; and I shall keep it unto the end. Give me understanding, and I shall keep thy law; yea, I shall observe it with my whole heart. Make me to go in the path of thy commandments; for therein do I delight."*

I understand this to mean that joy is found in following God's commandments and biblical precepts. But additionally, the flow of our joy comes from staying in the will of God. His commandments or precepts or laws all mean the same and will always reflect His will. Staying in God's precepts is where He gives us some insight into His will and His plan for our lives. Outside God's will will never invite joy because we can find ourselves outside of His plan for us. We were not outfitted for this worldly life outside of His plan. Understanding God's law from His perspective, not our own, and employing that law daily is the best way of staying in joy or, as the scripture indicated, "therein do I delight." Delight is joy and is used throughout the book of Psalm, most of which is believed to be written by David, to express his joy in prayer, psalm [celebration], and song to God. Our joy is in following God's word, which is the biblical law for the believer and Christ follower, but if we slip, God is faithful and just to forgive us as long as we ask Him with a heart of true repentance. Proverbs 29:18 (NLT) also confirms this point, "When people do not accept divine guidance, they run wild. But whoever obeys the law is joyful." We can see this happening now: folks running wild doing things they believe to be right, but they aren't even close. We need God's guidance provided through His word; His word is the law. Living outside of God's laws can lead to condemnation and shame as the devil will irrefutably bring up our sin since it is the nemesis to our faith and causes us to walk in fear. Following God's precepts keeps us in joy and clear from the devilish path of sin. God's commandments are not only found in the Bible. There are many things God has told us to do both audibly and inaudibly. Be advised that not following those commandments is just as important and the same as ignoring God's word. Let's examine the story of Adam and Eve again. God gave them a commandment not to eat of a specific tree in the Garden of Eden, which God pointed out to them so they didn't have to guess. Their joy was complete under the Adomic covenant as long as they followed God's commandment. We can infer that they had the fullness of joy because everything they needed was supplied for in the garden. However, the result of their disobedience and corruption toward God has led to a hard life of labor, which was never meant to be God's best and, I am sure, not as joyful. I can examine my own life and take notice of when I have obeyed the Holy Spirit and the consequence that ensued when I did not. I certainly wasn't joyful after and couldn't scapegoat on to God because He had already warned me through the Holy Spirit, who, by the way, is always ministering to us and advising, but we may not always be listening. For me, this was a simple situation of driving to work with a few minutes to spare but no time for stops or traffic jams. I heard the Holy Spirit tell me to take a different route, yet I thought I knew best and decided to take my usual route to work. I was working in a secular job then, and while I didn't have to punch a clock, it was still important to me to be timely, to set an example for my staff. Well, needless to say, I ran into traffic as a result of road work and ended up being twenty minutes late. To top it off, there was a directors' meeting that morning that I was running late to attend. I'm sure this situation could've been avoided had I heeded to the voice of the Holy Spirit. We make these kinds of mistakes, and sometimes the consequence is even greater depending upon the situation. We can make the same inference in the story of Peter when Jesus, God in the form of flesh, initially calls His disciples. This account can be found in Luke 5:3–11 (KJV). Jesus is testing Peter's faith, but I believe He was also looking to see if Peter would follow His commandment. Peter is asked to first thrust out a little from the land.

Then, when Jesus is done ministering, He tells Peter to launch out to the deep and let down his nets. Peter did question Jesus, as he says, "Master, we have toiled all night and have taken nothing," but he seemed to realize that the obedience to Jesus' word might yield great fruit, and his response continues, "nevertheless at thy word I will let down the net." Peter followed Jesus' commandment, and, as a result, he "enclosed a great multitude of fishes." Peter was astonished, and in some translations, the word "amazed" is used, or as in the NLT, it says he was awestruck at the draught of fishes. I believe he was awestruck with joy. After laboring all night, wouldn't you be overjoyed to finally accomplish your duty successfully? This is what he did for a living, so the impact on his business was great when he couldn't produce results from fishing. Yet Peter followed the word of Jesus once, and that's all he needed to believe and become a disciple of Christ forever. In that place of heeding to God's precepts, we can also find joy and many of the promises God wants us to claim. I implore you to keep and seek after all the commandments of the Lord your God (1 Chronicles 28:8).

The second scripture is in Psalm 16:11 (KJV), "You will show me the path of life; In Your presence is fullness of joy; At Your right hand are pleasures forevermore." The Holy Spirit showed me that by staying in His presence, there is overflowing joy as He shows me the path of my life. Conversely, if we are out of God's presence, we cannot conceive the path God has for our life, which could create frustration and a lack of joy. We cannot see the destiny of our life being outside of His presence. Sin, condemnation, shame, and other contaminated emotions can keep us out of the presence of God, but righteousness can lead us toward God's presence. Basking in the presence of God can expose us to a joy that is miraculous, overwhelming, and yet soothing. Regardless of circumstances, joy can be found by staying in His presence. We can stay in the presence of God by taking in God's Word in some form each day. Some may need it every hour of the day. Being in God's presence through prayer, praise, worship, reading the Bible, doing devotionals, and even symbolically recognizing the manifested presence of God can help us build relationship with Him. As a therapist, I have had many people share with me that the Bible is hard to understand, so that can be a barrier for why they don't read it. I would encourage you to choose a translation that is easier to comprehend, then invite the Holy Spirit to give you understanding and wisdom of His word. He will uncomplicate the complicated. Simply ask the Lord to make it plain. This is a way to keep us out of the presence of God by not reading His Word. Although we have to conceive at God's right hand, the hand of power and authority is pleasure, or, another way to say that, is joy forevermore. I interpret the right hand as a position of power and authority that we inherited by staying at God's right hand, as in staying in His presence. As we remain aligned with God at His right hand and in His presence, we can find joy. To expound on this point further, even the three wise men rejoiced at seeing the star [of David], which symbolized the birth of Christ, God in the form of His Son as the scripture indicated in Matthew 2:10 (KJV), "When they saw the star, they rejoiced with exceeding great joy." The three wise men recognized they were in the presence of God when they saw the star that led them to Christ, "the Governor, that shall rule my people Israel" (verse 6). We have to recognize the presence of God, Emmanuel symbolically, in miracles, and in all His embodiment. God's presence is omniscient, but when we talk about discovering joy in God's presence, we are referring to the manifested presence of God in our relationship with Him and His redemption for us. In Genesis, the Garden of Eden is the first place where God's presence is professed. The garden was God's sanctuary. Man first communed with God in His presence in the Garden of Eden, the place where the Creator and His creation had peace, joy, and supply. We have to stay in the presence of God because, in our relationship with Him, we can have everlasting joy!

The third pathway to finding joy can be found in Isaiah 51:3 (KJV),

> *"For the LORD shall comfort Zion: he will comfort all her waste places; and he will make her wilderness like Eden, and her desert like the garden of the LORD; joy and gladness shall be found therein, thanksgiving, and the voice of melody."*

God will comfort His people, the church. Joy and gladness, thanksgiving and a voice of melody, which is singing, can be found in the Garden of Eden created by our Lord, the original plan God had for us that was spoiled by the enemy. There is joy, peace, strength, no toiling, provision, godly wisdom, and more that can be found in the Garden of Eden. The etymology of Eden in Hebrew means "delight," but based on its Hebrew etiology, it can also be known as a place of *pleasure* or a land of *happiness*, fruitful and well-watered, as described in the Bible from various translations. It was described as an oasis (AMP Bible). The Garden of Eden, located where these four rivers, Pishon, Gihon, Hiddekel, and Euphrates, converge, was a type of heaven. Eden is a position of delight and tranquility and most closest to God, the epicenter of all creation and where our relationship was first established with Him. It's where God positioned man [Adam], and while he was in that position, he had the most dominance and authority; it was given to him by God (Genesis 1:26). During the fall, man lost his position of authority and surrendered power to Satan. However, Jesus came as the second Adam not only to save us from sin but also to restore our position with God along with our power and authority to function like God. That's what man was destined to do: act like God as we were created in His image and to imitate Him. We can take our authority back. That authority belongs to us to manifest joy on earth. As we stay in the Garden of Eden, we can also find our joy by being in a position closest to God and where everything is provided. Eden is a place for us to commune with God. It is our Christian philosophy and a mental ethos, the medicine for our mind. It's by communing with God that we can maintain a mindset focused on Eden. We were never meant to leave there. God has not asked us to leave Eden; the man [Adam] was asked to leave Eden, but our primary occupation is to stay fixed on Eden. God has made provision for the church to be comforted and have joy as we stay in Eden. The former Eden shall pass away, and the new sanctuary of God, that place of Eden, shall come into existence. As God prepares heaven and earth to be His own, He establishes a new Eden for us, even more beautiful than the first. It represents a place of joy, as is noted in Revelations 21:3–5 (KJV),

> *"And I heard a great voice out of heaven saying, Behold, the tabernacle of God is with men, and he will dwell with them and they shall be his people, and God himself shall be with them, and*

> *be their God. And God shall wipe away all tears from their eyes; and there shall be no more death, neither sorrow, nor crying, neither shall there be any more pain: for the former things are passed away. And he that sat upon the throne said, Behold, I make all things new."*

God is making a new Eden where there is no sin, affliction, or pain, and only the love of God remains. Fasten your attention to the italicized part of this scripture and imagine a place where there is no more death, sorrow, crying, pain—I would surmise that this could be defined as a place of joy where we can rejoice. Eventually, we will be in a place of eternal Eden, but until then, we have to stay in Eden in our spirit (the heart) and in our soul (the mind).

This next implementation of finding joy is not necessarily about the day itself but more a frame of mind. The fourth path to joy can be found in Isaiah 58:13–14 (NIV),

> *""If you keep your feet from breaking the Sabbath and from doing as you please on my holy day, if you call the Sabbath a delight and the Lord's holy day honorable, and if you honor it by not going your own way and not doing as you please or speaking idle words, then you will find your joy in the Lord, and I will cause you to ride in triumph on the heights of the land and to feast on the inheritance of your father Jacob." The mouth of the Lord has spoken."*

The Sabbath day is referred to as a "holy day" and a day of delight in some translations. And in some translations, the Sabbath is accredited as a "joyful day" or a "special day." If we pause in doing our own will on this holy day, then we will have joy in the Lord and ride upon the high places of the earth. The high places, to me, represent places of esteem and joy, unlike the low places, similar to a person feeling low, signify sadness and disgrace. Most people know and have come to understand the Sabbath represents a day of rest. The Christ followers are admonished to maintain the Sabbath, a day in time, but also understand what is expected of us on the Sabbath: rest—a moment to savor in the presence of God, to meditate on His Word, to make melody and rejoice, to put Him first and only Him. Some people have made a practice of doing the opposite, trying to stay busy or take action out of worry instead of resting in God. Sometimes, the best prescription is rest, that is, the action step. We have to build that skill to rest, perceiving it as the action we need to take instead of thinking we must do something. The Sabbath rest was built into our lives as a permanent prescription by God. Not just edifying the day of the Sabbath but maintaining a fervent disposition for the Sabbath can stir up joy in us. As I see it, we have to live the Sabbath day every day, and in so doing, God provides us with restoration from all our work, labor, and stress. The Sabbath day is first presented to us in Genesis 2:2. After God's creation week, He rested from speaking things into existence. On the seventh day was the day of rest. I don't believe this was added to this chapter to be prolific. It was intentional and significant for us to model after it. In verse 3, God blessed the seventh day and sanctified it because that was the day He rested from all His work. If God only spoke and rested on the seventh day, then we should shape ourselves after God's behavior. He formally gives this as an instruction to the Israelites, most notably as part of the ten commandments out of the 600-plus commandments that exist. Exodus 20:8–11 (AMP),

> *"Remember the Sabbath (seventh) day to keep it holy (set apart, dedicated to God). Six days you shall labor and do all your work, but the seventh day is a Sabbath [a day of rest dedicated] to the Lord your God; on that day you shall not do any work, you or your son, or your daughter, or your male servant, or your female servant, or your livestock or the temporary resident (foreigner) who stays within your [city] gates. For in six days the Lord made the heavens and the earth, the sea and everything that is in them, and He rested (ceased) on the seventh day. That is why the Lord blessed the Sabbath day and made it holy [that is, set it apart for His purposes]."*

The Sabbath day was made for us and our rest, not vice versa. After laboring for six days each week, it's necessary for our physical, psychological, and emotional well-being that we rest to spiritually connect with the one who gives us life daily. It's a day to refresh and rehabilitate those aspects of our being in order to strengthen our spiritual self. When the Israelites tried to collect manna from heaven on the seventh day, it was soured as God was testing their obedience to the law (Exodus 16:1–26). God was teaching the Israelites no longer to be enslaved to labor because they were no longer in Egypt but to trust Him by resting because the Sabbath is blessed and holy. Even they had to learn to respect the Sabbath. The Sabbath is a respite day and a gift from God that we should hold sacrosanct as a boundary for us to stay in the joyous repose God has for us. It is a day of delight, but as we maintain the sabbath attitude each day, we can feel invigorated and have pleasure. If you find yourself in Egypt, remind yourself to engage in a mental attitude consistent with the Sabbath day. We are no longer slaves or servants in Egypt (Deuteronomy 5:15) to anything, so we can rejoice for the freedom God has given us on the Sabbath day! You will find your joy in the Lord as you stay in an attitude consistent with the Sabbath rest.

The fifth pathway to joy is found in the presence of the angels of God. This parable really teaches us about the heart of God. Luke 15:10 (KJV) states, "Likewise, I say unto you there is joy in the presence of the angels of God over one sinner that repenteth." Jesus is ministering to a crowd of sinners and is overheard by Pharisees wishing to sabotage Him when He makes this declaration. In the scriptures preceding Luke 15:10, Jesus explains that if a woman who loses a coin rejoices over finding it, so should the angels rejoice over a sinner repenting. Angels are part of the universe God created and part of the angelic host of heaven, either visible or invisible, as Paul talks about in Colossians 1:16. Angels do rejoice when sinners become saints, and that transformation happens through genuine repentance. Since we are His disciples on this earth, then our goal should be to encourage sinners to repent, and as we do this, there is joy from the angelic host that we can also absorb. We can also participate in this joy by forgiving those who have wronged us so that they can have a fantastic encounter with God, hopefully leading them to sainthood. This commentary in Luke tacitly explains that sinners who repent become friends of Christ, and God is passionately overjoyed by one sinner who is saved. When we take part in that process by forgiving or walking in love toward someone who has sinned against us, we can also be blessed with joy by no longer being enslaved to bitterness and tied to resentment. We allow them to see the goodness of God in us, which can lead to a hunger in them to know Him more. That should bring us joy as well when those being used by the devil are now being used to do good; their goodness has an impact on us, also. However, the Holy Spirit gave me another interpretation of this scripture as well based on the first half— that joy is found in the presence of angels; thus, be mindful of the company you keep. We are not referring to the three types of angels found in the Bible, but more the character and spirit of a person [those we refer to as angels in their fleshly form based on their loving, heroic, or passionate actions of kindness]. Then, He added that those who are unrepentant could be of a foreign or demonic spirit. The Holy Spirit presented a very raw question to me, "Are you entertaining angels or demons?" However, angels and demons are all around us. I thought to myself, *This is a good observation, considering angels are from God and God represents everything good.* It's really a metaphorical question: am I entertaining those things that are good because what we entertain almost immediately becomes part of us and our thoughts? Joy is in entertaining those things that are good, and God has given us the wisdom to discriminate between good and evil because ambiguity may exist in what that looks like to us. We might not see the harm in something when God is trying to tell us we are entertaining demonic forces unaware. Then the Holy Spirit led me to 1 Corinthians 10:21 (KJV), "Ye cannot drink the cup of the Lord, and the cup of devils: ye cannot be partakers of the Lord's table, and of the table of devils." We cannot belong to God and to the devil. We have to want to be in the presence of angels, denoting those beings that are good or people who have repented and are genuinely living for Christ's good. As an alternative, we could end up in the presence of demons, indicative of all that is diabolical and evil. Hebrews 13:2 reminds us to be hospitable to strangers since we could be entertaining angels unaware. I believe God wants us to discern what type of spirit we are allowing ourselves to be around so that we can stay in the presence of angels and, therein, find joy. The devil is trying to reinforce the curse of sin and death through an attitude that is unrepentant. Do not be illiterate to the tactics of the enemy, particularly mentioned in John 10:10. God desires for us to repent and claim the joy He has for us, similar to the joy brought to Mary upon learning from an angel about the baby she would birth was to be the Savior of the world (Luke 1:26–38). God came in the form of flesh to secure our joy in Him and save us from sin. I would recommend allowing the Holy Spirit to minister to you about staying in the presence of angels. Additionally, I believe the foundation scripture is ministering to us as ambassadors for Jesus that we should be directly through serving others in love and indirectly through role modeling God's word, helping others come to repentance, and therefore accepting the grace gift of salvation. We are to preach the gospel of Jesus Christ, the Savior, and His anointing power to others. We have to demonstrate the need for living a repentant lifestyle, as angels rejoice as sinners make this transformation from sinners to saints. God has entrusted us and commissioned us to do this great work, as mentioned in the previous section. We have to decide whether we will take on this assignment, which, to me, is a dominant part of what God has called us to do and our purpose here on earth. As we help others repent and come to know the Lord, to be in personal relationship with Him, there is joy in the presence of angels. But we vicariously can experience that joy as well in doing God's work. Joy is in the conversion that happens while we minister to others. It is in knowing we have won one more over from the dark side. It's in growing our Christian family.

In Galatians 5:16–23 (KJV), we find the sixth passageway for discovering our joy.

> *"This I say then, Walk in the Spirit, and ye shall not fulfill the lust of the flesh. For the flesh lusteth against the Spirit, and the Spirit against the flesh: and these are contrary the one to the other: so that ye cannot do the things that ye would. But if ye be led of the Spirit, ye are not under the law. Now the works of the flesh are manifest, which are these; Adultery, fornication, uncleanness, lasciviousness, idolatry, witchcraft, hatred, variance, emulations, wrath, strife, seditions, heresies, envyings, murders, drunkenness,*

revilings, and such like: of the which I tell you before, as I have also told you in times past, that they which do such things shall not inherit the kingdom of God. But the fruit of the Spirit is love, joy, peace, long-suffering, gentleness, goodness, faith, meekness, temperance: against such there is no law."

The term "fruit" in the Bible has many meanings, both figurative and literal, and refers to the receipt of an investment or seed, a partnership with Christ, or the natural product of a thing. These nine fruits are the natural products consonant with the nature of the Holy Spirit, and we are asked to walk according to these things. These nine attributes should be held in reverence by every Christ follower and believer; they should be innate to our nature. Joy is a fruit of the spirit and the result of His fruit in us. It is the natural product of who God is. It's His heart. His presence in us allows the fruit of the spirit to germinate in us and continually produce more fruit, such as love, joy, peace, and all the other fruit mentioned. We can receive the fruit of joy by walking according to the Spirit of God in us. Likewise, walking after the things of the flesh, a lack of His presence in us could likely have negative consequences and a plethora of negative emotions attached to it. In the Merriam-Webster Dictionary, "joy" is defined most remarkably as "delight, pleasure, gladness." Joy is mentioned over 200 times in the Bible, depending on the translation, which demonstrates its importance and compelling nature as a fruit of the spirit. The fruit of the spirit is good and governs our walk as Christians here on earth. We are to be known by our fruit; thus, bearing these nine attributes demonstrates the God in us, the kingdom we serve, and His pure nature. This is not a mistake that joy happens to be a fruit of the spirit. In this scripture alone, I see a promise of God that we can benefit from the fruit of the spirit, but there is a request made on us first as you read further. We have to cling to, gravitate toward, strive after walking and living in the spirit. As verse 25 states, "If we live in the Spirit, let us also walk in the Spirit." Simply said, if we live in God's presence, let us walk as if His presence, His nature, is in us. You may want to ask yourself if you are living in the spirit with His presence in you, then you should be walking by His spirit. Jesus and

John the Baptist, not to be confused with the disciple yet a relative of Jesus, are the most proclaimed individuals in the Bible to follow after the fruit of the spirit prior to these nine godly traits being shared in Galatians. Jesus' life was a living example of walking after the fruit of the spirit, and the gospels are a representative of the fruit that He bore. Elizabeth mentioned to Mary how the babe in her womb leaped for joy when she learned of Mary's visit (Luke 1:44). John was leaping for joy and following after a fruit of the spirit from the womb. Let's briefly examine the story of Noah again. I believe Noah was also an example of someone who walked after the fruit of the spirit. In Genesis 6:9, Noah is referred to as a "just man and perfect in his generations, and Noah walked with God." First, he is called just. Then, he is referred to as perfect, not necessarily sinless—because nobody was perfect except Jesus—but complete and untainted. Then, the Bible says Noah walked with God. Thus, he wasn't walking against God. There was a maturity and a righteous spirit in Noah that he would be called to take on such an ardent yet amusing task to build an ark when flood waters had never come upon the earth. He and his family were spared out of, I am estimating, thousands of people who lived during that time. Why Noah? I believe because he was able to walk after the fruit of the spirit, submitting to the attributes of God based on His presence in Him instead of after the lust of the flesh as others were doing in that age. Walking after the fruit of the spirit is a choice, and as we make that choice to do so, God's divine and sovereign spirit will show up alongside us to sustain us. Against the tribulations and enticements of this world, God wants us to walk in the fruit of the spirit, bearing fruit analogous to His nature, I believe, just as Noah did. You have to let the fruit of the spirit, specifically joy, mature in you. The fruit of the spirit is in you, but you must relegate yourself to the Spirit so you fulfill the spirit walk and not the flesh walk. Walking after the flesh does not bring us joy. It is subject to the circumstances of our five senses. If the fruit of the Spirit is something you are striving for and the Spirit dwells in you, then joy should be following you instead of you chasing it as you recognize it as part of your nature gifted by God. Essentially, walking in the presence of God, which is walking in the spirit, is what enables us to experience God's presence in us. Then, we will not satisfy the lust of the flesh where joy does not exist. We are capable of bearing godly fruit consistent with the revelation we have by staying in the spirit. Joy is in you as a fruit of the Spirit, and since it's in you, you don't have to wait for circumstances to shift to receive joy. Take it because it is yours. If you are producing the fruit of joy in you, then you own it already. Since we are created in God's image, we do have His nature, and part of His nature is joy. Joy should be woven into the tapestry of who we are. It's part of our identity and image in God. It is the greatest souvenir we can possess to authenticate God's realness in our life.

The seventh place the Holy Spirit showed me to uncover joy is located in John 15:11 (KJV), "These things have I spoken unto you, that my joy might remain in you, and that your joy might be full." The things that Jesus is referring to in this scripture are that He is the true vine and we are the branches. Backing up to verses 4–5, Jesus counsels us to abide in Him and He in us since a branch cannot bear fruit without being attached to the vine. Then, He explains that He is the vine and we are the branches. As we abide one by another, we bear "much fruit." As I see it, Jesus is our source of joy as we stay connected to the source, the vine. Like a lamp plugged into a GI socket illuminates light, we can illuminate joy. The joy that Jesus speaks of in the aforementioned scripture cannot be found in earthly possessions, loved ones, our political affiliations, winning or losing, reaching our goals or not, wealth or a lack of wealth. Our joy remains full, as in a constant supply, by remaining connected to the vine. If you want to experience heavenly joy and the fullness of joy talked about in verse 11, then stay connected to the vine, the source of our joy. Practically, how can we stay connected to the vine? Verses 7 through 10 give us a prelude: (1) let His words abide in us—only speak Jesus-filled words, (2) continue in His love—know and accept His love for us and demonstrate His love, (3) keep His commandments to abide in His love, and thus we abide in the vine. He alone will fill us with all joy, as noted in Romans 15:13 (NIV), "May the God of hope fill you with all joy and peace as you trust in him, so that you may overflow with hope by the power of the Holy Spirit." We no longer have to be enslaved under the burden of depression and sadness. He is the God of all hope, and that hope in Him fills us with heavenly joy, but even this scripture suggests we have to stay connected to God in that we trust in Him. For me, trust implies connection. If there is no connection, how would you build trust? The God of hope fills us up, but do you believe in Him and trust Him? Are you connected to the vine where joy is produced, multiplied, and replenished? How much time are you spending with God to build trust in Him? No man has seen God, the Bible tells us, so in order to build trust, I need to spend time in Him, in His presence, in His nature, in His kingdom, the church. It's not the act of building trust with Him. It's in Him that we find our trust. In Him is the root of our joy. My joy is rooted and grounded in the Lord God Jehovah, the trinity of Him. It's not based on circumstances. It's based on my faith and love in Him. Though I cannot see Him now, I will see Him soon someday because I am connected to Jesus, the vine, and my branches continue to extend toward Him, the God of creation. No man can take that joy from me per John 16:22 (KJV). This life moves on a continuum from surviving to striving and then to thriving, but God wants us to thrive and live in the perfect and perpetual joy He has established for us. God established that fullness of joy for us before the foundation of the world and gave of Himself in the form of His Son for us to have that joy, but we have to be coupled alongside, connected to, or better yet in covenant with the source. Living with that kind of joy means maintaining our attachment to the vine. He is our link between the heavenly and earthly kingdoms and the only means for us to have joy here on earth. When I think about the story of Adam and Eve, both were at one point attached to the vine, but when they sinned, they not only fell from grace and lost their position with God, but they became detached from the vine. Adam specifically is a good example of what not to do if we are to walk in the goodness of God and remain attached to the vine, the source of our joy. Thinking about this scripture above and how I apply it during sessions with folks, I emphasize the three points highlighted, and then we review ways to stay attached to make this more of a pragmatic application and not just an allegory in a fun book to read for Christians that they will likely never get through. We can find a plethora of ways to stay attached to the vine, such as developing faith-based groups in your community and in the church that don't already exist. Creating a space in your house for quiet time, reflections, and devotion toward God's Word. The Bible is a tangible object for us to use in drawing close to God, particularly when we read it, but also having another object such as anointed oil, a prayer cloth, or something that ties you to God. In ancient biblical times, as part of the Hebrew culture, the Ephod was used to connect those in certain positions with God based on their priestly duties.

James 1:2–4 (NLT) states,

> *"Dear brothers and sister, when troubles of any kind come your way, consider it an opportunity for great joy. For you know that when your faith is tested, your endurance has a chance to grow. So let it grow, for when your endurance is fully developed, you will be perfect and complete, needing nothing."*

And so the eighth pathway to finding joy is when troubles come our way, as it's an opportunity for great joy. What does it mean by opportunity? I believe opportunity in this context means it's a chance for something new to happen or challenge you in an area to promote growth. Why is this an opportunity for joy? Because when our faith is tested through various tests, and that happens daily for some of us, then our endurance (or patience in some translations) is stretched, giving us a chance to mature. We receive fully developed patience, which allows us to achieve actualization through our Lord. That maturation is both spiritual and emotional. One aspect of life that we sometimes have a hard time embracing is growth, which cannot occur at times without challenging experiences stretching us. I like to refer to these experiences as opportunities instead of obstacles. You may scarcely be able to comprehend the various opportunities that came to challenge me while writing this book. The enemy was devotedly at work, but God's tenderness was greater, revealing His spiritual anatomy to me akin to the love He showed Jesus and giving me joy that was incomprehensible. He was composing His best performance in me by tapping on the windows of my spirit and reminding me that joy is found in these opportunities as it birthed in me moments to praise, glorify, and honor Him even more. While my faith was being tested, my endurance was growing. It grew through praise toward God and meditating on this scripture. It was an opportunity for fear or praise, and I chose the latter. Without realizing it, the enemy gave God's word a platform to work. I want to regularly be part of the James 1:22 generation. We can obtain great knowledge from reading God's Word and attending biblical classes and trainings, but that knowledge has to be applied, and that happens during these opportunities. That is what the Bible is supposed to be for us: a tool or weapon, the utilization of scripture to materialize whatever we need, whether a defense against the devil or daily prodigious encouragement. There is a scripture for everything. Imagine if we drank scripture like we drink coffee, tea, or whatever your guilty vice is. We would be fired up and ready to manage any troubles the enemy has targeted for us. Scripture is for revelation, direction, protection, provision, manifestation, and more. Jesus was referred to as a great teacher in scripture. It was revelation He received from His Father: any good teacher is going to test their students, and God is so loving He gives us multiple opportunities to test and retest even when we fail; that in itself should create joy. Or at least it's an opportunity for great joy for two reasons. Firstly, God is going to give us an opportunity to retest—the grace and love of God transmitted to us in a tangible way. Secondly, it's a chance for us to mature our patience. Thankfully, our God is not a God of one and done but provides multiple opportunities for us to learn and grow through spiritual testing. He also educates us prior to the test and typically will forewarn us when a test is about to happen. I want to say the Holy Spirit always foreshadows what is going to happen in advance, but we may not always be listening. The Bible is the main source of revelation on that, as per Psalm 34:19. We know the afflictions will come, and the Lord provides deliverance. Sometimes, it happens as a surprise, which has its benefits of not pre-stressing over something that you will not be able to change, but that is rare. God also gives us time warnings. The Bible might generalize it, but I know God has given me specific cautioning regarding events or will say I want you to increase your praise, prayer, double up on your offering, or even have me study a specific subject. I recall doing an intense study on grief three years ago, and I thought it was for the benefit of one of my therapy participants. I had no idea He had me studying on grief for me as preparation for when my beloved dog Buddy passed away and then, a year later, Bradley died. Regardless of the preparation or not, it is an opportunity for growth, which really depends on your response to it. Challenge yourself to have the right winning response, praise over fear. Let your endurance grow while testing your faith so that you can be perfect and complete, not perfect like Jesus but whole, needing nothing. Look at these situations as opportunities for joy because, from that view, you can achieve so much more but also put yourself in a position of being positive instead of viewing life as a pessimist. Every test doesn't have to be viewed as something negative happening to us when, in reality, it's God showing us His excellent love in a way that maybe we don't even realize. We are not victims, but only in our skewed perceptions of reality is our victim nature made real. This is a distorted perception by the devil. Don't believe it. Refuse to accept any victim mentality by speaking faith-filled words over it. Then, change your perception. What loving parent doesn't educate their children, challenge them, and then correct them? God does all three, and He does it in such a way that we are provoked to change and challenged in our faith, but in the end, we can arrive at a place of loving Him more. We don't have to be fearful when tests come if we understand the opportunity that comes from drawing nearer to God during these moments and learning to mature our patience. It is, as James says, an opportunity for genuine joy.

The ninth way to finding joy is to never burn out but stay fueled in God's Word. "Don't burn out; keep yourselves fueled and aflame. Be alert servants of the Master, cheerfully expectant. Don't quit in hard times; pray all the harder. Help needy Christians; be inventive in hospitality" (Romans 12:11–13, MSG). "Cheerfully" in this scripture can be translated as joyfully being expectant. You could replace that word, and the scripture would read the same way. Expectant of what? I think we need to be expectant of all things, whether good or bad. As previously explained, we can understand that all things that aren't good or evil are from the devil. Let's be very clear on this point: he is the source of all things negative and evil. However, that doesn't mean that God cannot use something that was meant for evil for our good. God might authorize these happenings like He tested Job, but He will never give us more than we can bear, nor will He allow us to fail if we trust Him explicitly (Proverbs 3:5–6). He wants us to succeed, but He also has to challenge us in ways that will expand our faith and trust in Him. Do not be conned in believing that God causes us to fail or allows bad things to happen to hurt us. He is never the source of evil, only good, as previously mentioned. However, as Christ followers, we need to understand that we are not greater than our master, the great teacher Jesus. If Jesus endured all the physical suffering and pain that He did, we are definitely no better than Him. We should also be willing to endure for the sake of the cross, for the love that Jesus Himself demonstrated for us, evidenced by giving His life and the grace gift we now have since we have been reconciled back to our heavenly Father. Expectation of those things that aren't so good allows us the opportunity to "not quit and pray all the harder," being "fueled and aflamed" per the base scripture. Don't quit in hard times tells me that hard times are to be expected, but it is an opportunity, not an obstacle. Let's dissect this scripture further because the first part gives us some direction, "don't burn out," which is huge for all of us because of how many of us are burning ourselves out, constantly giving to others but never filling ourselves up. Working multiple jobs is based on financial circumstances, but it's causing you to burn out. Taking on more assignments than you should, trying to cope or avoid something. Some folks are running on fumes, not fuel, so, of course, you cannot experience the joy God has for you. I am not going to go on a diatribe about the importance of rest because there are enough resources about that on the market. However, we do need to understand that if our joy is not at a place where we want it, ask yourself if you are burnt out. The second directive is to stay fueled and aflamed. How often are you staying aflame and fueled by God's spirit in you? I know, as a therapist, I am giving of myself six days a week, which can deplete my energy not just physically but spiritually and mentally, so I stay fueled in my devotional time with God. I need that time with Him to feed my spiritual person and also mentally cleanse myself from the day-to-day emotions that I could carry as a result of vicarious trauma. I cannot sleep away mental exhaustion, so if I don't stay attuned to God's Word, I can certainly find myself less tolerant, more irritable, and less compassionate. To maintain my fervor in the practice and my passionate joy for what I do, it is a must for me that I am fueling daily. Just as I eat daily, I have to feed daily on God's Word. Now, feeding our spirits can look different for each person; it can be reading chapters in the Bible, listening to a sermon and taking notes, or even authentic praise and worship. There are many ways to feed your spirit, including fasting, prayer, communion, meditating on scripture, reading books authored by faith-based citizens of heaven, but I like to get into the word because scripture, for me, is fuel to my spirit and soul. It pleases God when we read His word as it's training for our spirit to be like Him and a responsive demonstration of our covenant relationship with Him. However, if I am trying to work out a negative emotion I am feeling, I have found authentic praise and worship have been successful for me. Because, as a therapist, it is inevitable that we will carry some of the heart-throbbing emotions that come from offering therapy to others, finding cathartic release is helpful. I can't hold on to that "stuff." I find it toxic and noticed for a long time when I did that it was hindering my ability to be fully present and helpful to my therapy participants. Over the years, I have learned whatever I am feeling, I know that I can lean on my faith for fuel so I am not burning out. If I don't know what to do with the emotion I am feeling, I always go to God in prayer; it is my default method for finding resolution—it's the seeking Him first approach. Many times, my prayer will start off as a conversation with God, transitioning to my heavenly prayer language before actually going into covenant prayer. The third step is to be alert servants of the master. I see that as God wants us to listen to, acknowledge, and adhere to Him. Are we attuned to God, and do we recognize His voice? Can we hear Him when there is a lot of rhetoric going on in our head? If you find yourself not being alert, then look for ways to connect to Him. As you stay alert and connected to Him, your joy will return. We already talked about the importance of staying connected to Him, and there are many avenues to allow for that to happen, a few previously noted. The last part of this scripture is about helping needy Christians and being inventive in hospitality. I see that as engaging in altruistic behavior. Being able to do for others in need and being congenial is a nice backdrop for fueling our joy. The Bible calls us to be cheerful givers. I am going to use the word joyful givers (2 Corinthians 9:7). We aren't to give out of necessity or grudgingly, but as we purposed in our heart, give. That type of giving is an offering to God and to others. We can share the God in us with others through our giving. And so when you smile, let that be an offering in the spirit of joy to someone else.

The goal is not to view these nine pathways as a formula for finding or obtaining joy. However, what is predominantly demonstrated is that our joy comes from our covenant partnership with God through our salvation, and many of the scriptures aforesaid explore how our joy can be more perfected and maintained. It must be a lifestyle practice, not a temporary process. Look at these scriptures as an agreement we have with God. Don't change the terms of the joy agreement by doing something contrary to what you read in scripture. The problem with many of us is that we have tried to change the terms by looking to achieve joy in this world, which doesn't offer us the satisfaction we are looking for. Money doesn't bring joy, the best car, designer clothes, the biggest house, and so on. When you chase after these things in an effort to achieve joy, you have missed the mark. You changed the terms of the agreement, but the Bible has been clear all along on where we find joy and how to receive it. Nothing should be able to separate us from this joy as we remain in love with our heavenly Father. Our happiness can change from season to season or by circumstance to the next circumstance, but joy is not fulfilled by circumstance, seasons, possessions, or even experiences. It remains anchored to our relationship with God. I learned only a few years ago that my joy cannot be complete without a relationship with Him. As long as I've been a Christian, one would think I should have known this, but that's a good illustration of the fact that, as Christ followers, we are always learning. We have to be receptive to learning. Let me assert this point again: the closer we are to God, the source for our very existence, the greater the joy we may receive. If you become spiritually disconnected from Him, then your joy will be adversely affected. Notice that all the scriptures above point back to a strong connection to God and His word; thus, our joy is from Him, not a formula or a recipe. However, we can use the scriptures in this chapter as a way to rediscover our joy when we find ourselves lost in an emotional state of grief and joylessness. Responding to these nine scriptures is both a pathway of direction and a passageway of entry to finding your joy. We take these scriptures, the Word, as the antidote for joylessness. It should be a way of life as we are expected to live by the Word of God, as Jesus made this proclamation to the enemy while being tempted in the wilderness. "But he answered, 'Man shall not live by bread alone, but by every word that proceedeth out of the mouth of God'" (Matthew 4:4, KJV). What does that mean, living by every word that proceedeth out of the mouth of God? Let's first look at what is considered God's word. The Bible is the primary source of God's word. It is a compilation of lyrical poems, holy writings, letters, and consecrated teachings in messianic story form to provide a history of Judaeo-Christian culture and doctrine as an example for us, along with providing an expectation of what is to come. Anything deviating from the Bible, including any teaching, is not God's word. And those who are ministering according to God's Word are first disciples of God, then part of the ministry gifts as tutored by Paul in Ephesians four. Secondly, why live by His Word? We, who are Christ followers, should understand that God's Word contains both power and authority. It is energetically life-giving, vigorously loving, and yet forceful enough to shut the mouth of the enemy. Notice Jesus did not succumb to the temptation in the wilderness, somewhat of a parallel process to what the Israelites experienced in the wilderness; however, less successful. He shut the mouth of Satan by speaking God's Word only. The enemy came to test him, and he regurgitated God's Word back to him. I have had therapy participants almost question why we should repeat God's Word to Satan when he knows it. Correct, he knows the Word, and he wants to know if you will acknowledge God's Word and apply God's Word to your situation. Jesus knew the Word and applied it to His situation. And we also have to know that Satan likes to distort the Word. The true test is, what do you know about God's Word, and what are you willing to apply it to? The demonic assaults come to bring us further away from the Word. It's designed to steal our joy by pushing us further away from our position to God. The New Testament brings to us a profound joy in the life of Jesus as a sample disciple of God, His beloved, and the well-pleasing one, the rabbi, the Son of God, the Son of Man, our Savior, and the adjudicator of our damnation bringing us back to the Father in faith and righteousness, and thus our joy is consummated in connection to the Holy Trinity: Father, Son, and Holy Spirit. The Trinity provides the disposition to our joy and the reason to smile. We are not alone in this life, and whenever we find ourselves detached from our heavenly joy, we should know the direction back to it. However, we have to know it's not only the joy that comes from the Trinity but the joy that stems from having faith in the Trinity of our monotheistic God and exercising that faith in any circumstance. We exercise our faith in connection to living by the Word that proceedeth out of the mouth of God. The most important question is, how can we exercise faith if we don't understand what we have faith in? Many folks talk about the triune being of God, but they have no idea what each part does. It is akin to how Paul describes the church; we are all many members, but one body, first seen in Romans 12:4–5 and repeated again in 1 Corinthians 12:12–13. It's not enough to have the knowledge of the Father, His Son, and the Holy Spirit. We need to understand each individual function that they hold so that our faith is more effective. There is a trichotomy with God, but all three parts are acting as one. In the beginning was God, as Genesis indicates in chapter one, verse 1, "In the beginning God"; thus, we know it started with Him. His Son, Jesus, doesn't show up in the flesh until the New Covenant in the Bible, what we refer to as the New Testament; however, we know Jesus was with God in the beginning, as described by John in the Gospel of John 1:1 (KJV), "In the beginning was the Word, and the Word was with God, and the Word was God." The "Word" is emblematic of God's Son, Jesus. He existed in the beginning in the form of the spirit but comes in the form of the flesh to establish the New Covenant. In his book *The Power of the Blood Covenant: Uncover the Secret Strength of God's Eternal Oath*, Malcolm Smith defines covenant as "a binding, unbreakable obligation between two parties, based on unconditional love sealed by blood and the sacred oath that creates a relationship in which each party is bound by specific undertakings on each other's behalf." He further explains this covenant is mediated by the Lord Jesus and established by His blood. The covenant is sealed by the Holy Spirit, who helps us to live out our part of the covenant by establishing God's law in our hearts. And scripture tells me God is the author and witness of the covenant. As you can see, all parts of the Trinity have a role. While reading Genesis, I happened to glance over the language and understand that it is different than the semantics we use today. However, I thought it was very interesting to find that Genesis 1:26a states, "And God said, Let us make man in our image, after our likeness." I choose to believe that the "us" and "our" in this sentence are crediting Jesus in His physical absence and not yet introduced to mankind but exist in the stratosphere, the realm of the unseen. This is also intimated in Isaiah 48:16, which states that Jesus was not present in secret. He existed from the beginning. Then, we have the Holy Spirit, who shows up in the New Covenant after Jesus' crucifixion but was prophesied about by Jesus ahead of time and also existed from the beginning. In John 14:16–26, Jesus talks about the Comforter He asks God to send to the disciples. As disciples today, we have the same Comforter with us. The Holy Spirit comes in the name of Jesus to provide us with intelligence, wisdom, knowledge and to be a reminder of what we have previously learned in an effort to keep the covenant. And so God is the head, Jesus is the arbitrator and blood sacrifice on our behalf, and the Holy Spirit is the Comforter and Guide. As we know this, we can pray to God the Father through faith in His Son Jesus and receive knowledge from the Holy Spirit on how to pray and know that whatever we pray for...it is done. You can pray for joy; just know that holding onto the aforesaid scriptures where joy has been inaugurated is the best way to experience God's joy. Moreover, by having an understanding of the Trinity in context to our heavenly joy, we can recognize what we have faith in and how to exercise that faith more effortlessly.

Chapter 5

Smile: We Aren't Victims but Conquerors

My joy can come from knowing that I am a conqueror in Christ Jesus. The Bible refers to us as more than conquerors through Jesus, who loved us (Romans 8:37), and the authority we have over the enemy (Luke 10:19) also reminds us that we are more than conquerors in Jesus' name. We have to be in a position to overcome something to be more than a conqueror. Thus, something is likely going to happen that will cause us to be more than a conqueror. Don't act like it's a surprise when that something comes. It's just forcibly pushing you to be more than a conqueror, more importantly, an overcomer. The name of Jesus provides us with authority and power over the enemy to even slaughter him in warfare when necessary. Put on your spiritual armor as noted in Ephesians 6:10–20, or as David did against Saul. Only then can you be more than a conqueror. David is being threatened with death by his predecessor, but God was always there protecting him, and he never had to lay a hand on Saul to defend himself though having the opportunity to do so and being in close proximity while in the cave. He cuts a portion of Saul's robe but nothing further, as he sees Saul as "his master and the Lord's anointed." And he also forbade his servants to rise up against Saul (1 Samuel 24:1–7). Saul was a strong warrior who chased David from high lands to low lands, but David kept his joy. David was destined for greatness from the beginning, and he was viewed as more than a conqueror, as described in 1 Samuel 17 when he challenged Goliath without fear. When nobody else believed he could defeat this nine-foot-plus giant, he believed he could. Saul doubted saying he is "but a youth" or, in some translations, saying he's only a boy. Those thoughts were defeatist type thoughts. David met Saul's words with a disclosure of victory against a lion to protect his father's livestock. To be a conqueror, we have to think like a conqueror but also be willing to match any doubt with words of victory. David showed immeasurable strength, never giving up his joy even in the face of what seemed like formidable opponents. What is most important in these chapters is that David never perceived himself as a victim but was always humble first to God, and then he became victorious. The devil doesn't have the power to possess your joy unless you let him. Don't give him that power to laden you with thoughts of victimhood and doubting your confidence in God's Word. His Word says we are more than conquerors, and we have to believe it to be so. David was a servant of God and heard His voice. Only during these opportunities was he able to grow his faith and strengthen his relationship with the Almighty God. He only spoke faith words and never gave up his power. David has his faults, but he also recognized the humility that comes from being obedient to God's Word. David is a perfect example of several of the pathways for discovering joy previously noted as he followed God's precepts, stayed connected to the vine, stayed in His presence, had many troubles come his way, yet remained fueled and aflame, fervently expectant. If you have mistakenly given up power to the enemy, you do have the right to take it back by being obedient and speaking the word only, just as the centurion communicated to Jesus, indicating he didn't need Jesus to come to his servant's home. He only needs to speak healing words (Matthew 8:5–13). We need great faith like that centurion to just speak the Word. This is chronicled in the Bible as a story of great faith, the type of faith God would like for us to possess that is restorative and resilient. Be like the centurion as he told Jesus to "speak the Word only and my servant will be healed." Speak joyful words only and you will have joy. But the words we speak must be spirit-filled, righteous words in faith. In his book *Faith and Confession*, Charles Capps emphasizes on speaking faith-filled words as he indicates two faith secrets in working the law of seed time and harvest: "1) faith works like a seed, and 2) the way to plant it is to say it." He goes on to explain that "the words you are speaking, even when you are not confessing the Word of God, should be in agreement with the Word of God." This means that you need to speak joyful words that are congruent with God's word even when scripture is not being quoted, such as words of affirmation, positive statements pertaining to joy. Everything you say should be reflecting God's word. Regardless of what you are going through or the struggles you have experienced in the past or maybe presently, your faith in Christ can make you whole again. "Whole" in that there is nothing missing and nothing lacking in your life—a wholeness synonymous with heavenly joy. God restored Job, Jesus restored Lazarus, God restored Jesus, and that same miracle working power is able to restore us supported by the Holy Spirit. Let your faith in God restore joy in your life by speaking words compatible with God's word, then speak it out with power and authority, believing what you say. I tend to favor scripture because I am a firm believer in God, honoring His Word, which liveth and abideth forever (1 Peter 1:23b), but you have to do what feels authentic to you based upon how you best receive. However, ensure whatever you do favors God's Word. By speaking the Word, we prove ourselves to be more than conquerors in Christ. We are more than conquers made in the image of God and have been redeemed from the hand of the enemy. Declare it, as noted in Psalm 107:1–2. The Message says it this way (verses 1–2): "Oh, thank God—he's so good! His love never runs out. All of you set free by God, tell the world! Tell how he freed you from oppression." God's love is abundant toward us, and He has freed us from oppression so we are not oppressed. Remind yourself and others that you are not oppressed. Circumstances come to test our perseverance in our faith, but we are not oppressed. The devil is trying to hurt us, but we are not oppressed. The devil may use agents of this world to come against us, but we are not oppressed. We can still have great joy in God's resurrection power to redeem, restore, and provide resilience so that we know we are not oppressed. Your initial response to the enemy determines the fervor at which he comes after you. Your response needs to be: You are more than a conqueror with godly joy. Do not let the devil tell you anything contrary to this truth: "You are not a victim but a conqueror." That's it, period. Amen.

How do we know that we are conquers? We have to change our thoughts, and we can do that by refreshing our heart and mind in the Word of God. In the Old and New Testaments, the spiritual mind is used to reference the heart intentionally because what is in the heart becomes imprinted in our minds and will come out of our mouth. We have to change what we say, and that only happens by transposing our thoughts for God's thoughts. I believe that as you change your thoughts, you can change the level of your joy. The Bible says in Proverbs 23:7a (KJV), "As a man thinks in his heart so is he." We have to change our thinking so we know we are conquerors. You can convince yourself you are a conqueror by refreshing your thinking through scripture that tells you who you are in Christ Jesus. The Bible tells us to renew our inward man, the Spirit, day by day (2 Corinthians 4:17). We are going to encounter and hear junk contrary to our Christian ideology that tells us we are not more than conquerors, and that's why it is vitally important for us to refresh our heart and mind by cleansing ourselves with the word of God daily. Just as we clean our physical bodies daily, we have to clean our spiritual mind. We can cleanse our minds by showering ourselves using kingdom principles found in God's Word. It serves as a reminder of who we are and what we are capable of in the name of Jesus. I want to examine a couple of scriptures that further illustrate who we are and how we should maintain in this world. The following is a great scripture to meditate on as a way to manifest our victory in this world. "But thanks be to God, which giveth us the victory through our Lord Jesus Christ" (1 Corinthians 15:57, KJV). God gives us victory through our relationship with Jesus. He did all He's going to do at the cross, but the victory comes through relationship, so we have to accept a relationship with Him. That may not seem intelligible for us to comprehend, particularly when going through the challenges and opportunities in life, causing us to question our victory. How do we know we are victorious by going through struggles? Because Jesus prophesied persecutions would come but admonished us to hold fast to God's Word. We have to know God gives us victory in spite of afflictions. Meditate on this verse by personalizing it and maybe say it daily for a while until you begin to believe it. All of the Word of God works through our faith and belief. As we continue repeating scripture as a form of meditating on God's Word, it ministers to our heart faith and strengthens our belief. It acts like a cleansing cloth to our spirit. Be washed by the Word, and then praise the Lord that you are victorious! Only repeat that and nothing else as the enemy tries to use the words of our mouth and insert negative thoughts in our mind to harm us. What we think and meditate on will eventually be excreted from our mouth. Yes, I equated it to excrement because, for some of us, what comes from our mouth is that. Don't speak from a place of temptation, frustration, or anger about your situation, as it gives the enemy power. Our life is a reflection of what we think and say. If you don't like the lack of joy in your life, start thinking and speaking differently. Don't give up your power. "Don't burn out; keep yourselves fueled and aflame. Be alert servants of the Master, cheerfully expectant. Don't quit in hard times; pray all the harder. Help needy Christians; be inventive in hospitality" (Romans 12:11–13, MSG). I feel like this scripture provides so much encouragement but also gives us firm instructions not to give up, to stay fueled in the Word of God, to be alert for the enemy and cheerful in all situations, to help those in need, and to be welcoming. I believe that as we demonstrate altruistic behaviors toward others, we can't be sad. I don't know about other folks, but I find it hard to give to others with a sour puss look on my face. Actually, as we cheerfully give, we embolden and reinforce the spirit of joy. Giving is another way to release our joy for victory. We have to believe and receive it in our spirit that we are not victims if we don't quit and if we don't burn out. We need to feast on scriptures like the aforementioned one, which fuels us during challenging and changing times. Meditate the goodness of God's Word about who you are. In 1 John 4:4 (KJV), the Bible tells us, "Ye are of God, little children, and have overcome them: because greater is he that is in you, than he that is in the world." We are of God and belong to Him. That alone allows us to be victorious, but He doesn't stop there. He calls us His little children, and we have overcome them, which is the world and the antichrist in the world. However, this scripture expressly says the God in us is greater than the antichrist and the agents of darkness in this world.

God didn't leave us helpless. He gave us the Holy Spirit as a comforter to help us live this life. Some people refer to the Holy Spirit as it or something. As I've heard the statement, something told me to…I kept hearing it say. "He's not something or an it." The Holy Spirit is an intelligent gentleman and a real, living immortal being. He resides in us, but we need to utilize Him, develop Him in us, or resurrect Him, as some of us have buried Him like treasure. He is a treasure, but not to be entombed. Exercise Him and accept His direction for your life because therein we can smile. We all need the education, influence, and guidance of the Holy Spirit. The metrics of our joy can also be seen in how much we utilize the Holy Spirit. Since the Holy Spirit lives in us, we are more than conquerors. Greater is He that lives in us than he that is in the world—if we believe this scripture, then we have to do things congruent with this scripture: 1) act like you believe it and quit thinking your joy comes from circumstances being better or people liking you. God likes you. Even better, He loves you. You have to know that the God in you is greater than what this world has to offer you or what this world tries to preach to you. Use the God in you to cause circumstances to change. It might take time, but the more fervent your faith in Him, the quicker the circumstances might shift, or your perception of the situation might be transformed. I believe God appreciates the latter more than the antecedent. Don't accept junk. Ardently keep meditating on this scripture without giving up or becoming discouraged. Put a smile on your face and dance on the devil in the middle of challenges and opportunities. 2) You have to live like the one in you [God] is greater. We quote this scripture but don't recognize the true power in it. As Christ followers, we should understand the strength and might that this scripture has conveyed to us, and for others who are struggling with their Christian walk, you may have to use rote review of this scripture before your faith can grasp hold of it and you start to believe it. That may take more time for some, but it depends on how pliable you are with letting God's word infiltrate your heart and mind. It needs to penetrate through the junk you have filled your heart and mind with from this world. But God is greater than this world, and He dwells in us in the form of the Holy Spirit as long as we have accepted His Son as Lord of our lives. Greater is He that is in you than any problem you face or challenge that comes your way, or opportunity that God gives you than what the world has to offer you. Greater is He that is in you than the situation trying to steal your peace and joy. Greater is He that is in you than the demonic agents of the enemy trying to steal your smile. Greater is He that is in you than the persons pretending to be your friend. Greater is He that is in you than the churchgoer who is not a Christ follower. Greater is He that is in you than the anger that engulfs you or the tears that flow down your face. Greater is He that is in you always! Lean on the Greater One during challenging times. After all, that is what He has asked us to do. We are of God per this same scripture, so we have to act like we come from Him. We have the same DNA and thus the same abilities to manifest all that God has for us, including the joy He predestined for us to receive. Smile in the face of unpromising and unfavorable circumstances as you recognize that greater is the one in you than he that is in the world. Your attitude has to be I have a right to everything that Jesus died on the cross for me to have. Joy is one of those gifts that His death and subsequent resurrection gave us, and He dwells in you now in the form of the Holy Spirit. He is the gateway to our joy and peace. When I need to quarantine myself from worldly anarchy and absurdity, I expose and surrender myself to God. I exercise the Holy Spirit, not exorcise, but exercise as in "put to use" versus "expelling Him." Pull on the Holy Spirit to guide you and encourage you through this earthly kingdom and the forces of evil in this world. The greater one is in you!

We cannot live this life alone. We do need help spiritually and sometimes naturally. The Holy Spirit can provide us with spiritual encouragement, and we have to pull on Him for what we need. He might say to us to tune into this faith-based show or movie, watch this Christian broadcast, listen to that gospel song, read that scripture. Then,

He ministers to us through that resource specifically on what we need at that moment. The Holy Spirit can provide wisdom and encouragement to us through many avenues. When we do become disheartened by whatever is happening in our lives, just know we can find hope in the Holy Spirit, who will lead us to and through God's Word to bring us insight in whatever format we learn the best. If it's through reading, the Bible might be the source He uses, and He may lead you to a scripture that leaps off the page to you and resonates with your spirit man. Sometimes, we need reassurance in the natural, and God sends us people who will help encourage us and be invariably empathetic. We can ask God to surround us with people who will minister, encourage, and strengthen our spirit. Sometimes, we do need that in the natural. I think about what a smile and a hug do for me when I am in a space of need. Yet I have learned to lean on God's word and the Holy Spirit when encouragement isn't possible in the natural. Having other Christ followers to lean on is wonderful; however, balance that because we are not a leech on other people, the primary means of our encouragement should come from God's Word and through the Holy Spirit. Everything we need is in His word, and by following that word, we can be more than conquerors.

The Bible iterates the preponderance of who we are supposed to be and how we are to act in our faith. Those who have comprehended this Christ walk for many years have understood we are not supposed to lie down and take cheap shots from the enemy. We possess our joy, and that can't be taken from us unless we surrender it. As believers, we have to stand strong in our faith, and for some, they seem to believe that because they are Christians, they are not to be warriors. Yes, we are to walk in love, but that is one weapon for battle. There are many more, such as maintaining our strong faith, fighting with joy, smiling, using the sword of the word, and more. Our faith should be progressive, operative, and our leading weapon against the darkness of this world. We are not quitters. We don't shirk our responsibilities to fight off the devil, hide our weapons during war, or go trembling into battle. We fight triumphantly. But we do need to know what weapons to use during various situations.

First Timothy 6:12 (NLT) prompts us to “fight the good fight for the true faith. Hold tightly to the eternal life to which God has called you, which you have declared so well before many witnesses.” I perceive that Paul is telling Timothy that we are in battle, as the word “fight” indicates that notion. If in battle, we shouldn’t be cowards but make sure we are bearing arms with our fellow believers in Christ for the joy that God has promised us. Your smile shouldn’t be impacted by waging war against the enemy because, one, we know our smile is a weapon, and secondly, we already know the outcome of this battle: we win. The only way we don’t win is by abandoning our faith and conceding to the devil. Those who are Christ followers should be fighting the good fight for the true faith, not just any faith, but the faith that brought us back in right standing with God. Then, we are to hold tightly to the eternal life to which God has called us, the eternal life that brings us joy.

Chapter 6

The Difference between Joy and Happiness

Have you ever wondered if there is a difference between joy and happiness? I certainly believe there is, and there is value in recognizing the disposition between the two. Happiness can be achieved on your own and a sensation driven by circumstances that impact our senses in such a way that it produces a laugh or a smile. It is contingent upon external happenings in our environment. Happiness is part of the Babylonian system. I have learned to interpret that as a system that tries to replicate God's promises in the Word by rejecting His instruction through the willfulness and idolatry of man. Simply stated, happiness is the idea of trying to meet your need for joy without God. The Israelites were momentarily happy upon exiting Egypt, but that quickly dissipated once in the wilderness as they began murmuring and complaining about their surmisable lack, though God promised to take care of them. Their external circumstances changed, and it impacted their level of happiness, which was motivated by superficially and conditionally based circumstances. Their joy would've been discovered by recognizing that our God, Jehovah the Provider, will supply their needs through staying in a place of Eden, having a sabbath attitude, and staying in the presence of God. Unfortunately, their happiness was short-lived. Happiness is manufactured by the enemy to mimic the genuineness of joy. Joy is attainable through your faith and hope in God. It's not based on circumstances because circumstances are ever-evolving, just as it was for the Israelites. It's the same for us. Greater joy comes from greater faith. How you respond to your measure of faith will determine your level of joy. Joy is the God-given goodness inside of us that is sustainable regardless of circumstances and is predicated on being an unconditional emotion. Joy is contagious and is endowed with magnetism, rubbing off easily toward others, while happiness is exclusively surface-deep. Happiness is only present during tough mitigating circumstances or an inflation of optimistic circumstances. The Israelites' mood was up and down all the time—angry with Moses at times, and at other times, Moses was their hero. Their happiness was demonstrated by external incentives and defined by their emotional stability. They are not alone, as all of us have likely found ourselves up and down at times based on our circumstances instead of accepting the peace and joy God commissioned for us. The devil will bring up circumstances not only as a distraction but to keep us out of a place of praise and worship, gratitude toward God, and even sometimes push us further from His will. Yet, in His will is where we find joy. In the perfect plan of God, there is overflowing joy. We allow circumstances to dictate our faith and love walk toward God, influencing the joy He wants us to experience. Anger can certainly distance us from the full joy of God, and the enemy knows this, which is why the goal is to affect the soundness of our environment. The devil strategically places bumps in the road for us to trip over, but the Bible reminds us that when we fall, God picks us up. Thankfully, God will love us in spite of our attitude toward Him, and He has proven that over and over, but we have to understand our joy should not be provisional. Joy is intrinsically motivated, while happiness is motivated by seeing outside the self that things in our environment are going well. I may be unhappy some days, but my joy never changes. Why? Because of my walk with Jesus, my love for Him, and the fact that I will get to spend eternity with Him make me joyful. This is not it. This life on earth is not the end for us, who are Christ followers. If we have a close relationship with God, our joy is in knowing that this, too, shall pass. Whatever the situation is that you're facing is temporary. Our joy is a fruit of the spirit, a gift from God. Moreover, it can remain full as we stay connected to the source of our joy and respond in faith to each situation that comes up. It gives us the strength to move forward in spite of the situation before us or the chaos going on around us. Happiness is not long-lasting and eventually will fade. Joy is rechargeable by renewing our mind in God's Word, which is why we are admonished multiple times throughout the Bible to do so. We can also recharge our joy by maintaining an attitude of Sabbath rest, staying in the stillness of God, along with being at peace with Him. If anger comes up, please know that it is not God's desire for you, and remaining angry with God about your situation will prevent you from experiencing His joy just as it prevented first-generation Israelites from going into the Promised Land, the place of their joy.

Joy is from God. It is achievable, and it's a habitual feeling for those in the faith. Whatever the circumstance is, it won't last forever. Don't think it will. Weeping is for a night only, meaning it's momentary, but joy is coming in the morning. This does not denote the time of day but rather specifies that sadness won't last forever. We all can have joy as long as we stay connected to the vine through which our joy can be found. Though our outward disposition might be temporarily doleful and distressed, our inner predisposition should be one of maintaining a strong courage that demonstrates our endurance in God's word, that we can have hope and joy. Position yourself for praise to give God the glory through the circumstance, as it will change your outer disposition and your perception of the situation to one of hope and joy. Joy is constant, and although the circumstances look grim, our heart mood should be unchanging. God couldn't do enough to make the Israelites happy. Their happiness was insatiable, and that is another defining factor for happiness versus joy. If nothing and nobody can do enough to make you happy, then you don't possess joy. Joy is part of the kingdom of God. It is a spirit of joy, promised to us by the acceptance of His Son, and we can receive it by faith. The ability to smile through the storms of life is through joy. Having joy can bring us into a place of happiness, not that the circumstances have changed, but you have divorced yourself from embracing a negative response to the situation. Or reflecting on God's heavenly joy has altered your perception regarding the situation. You may be going through the worst time of your life and still maintaining joy; only God can provide us with that type of sensation, joy unspeakable. The ability to laugh, though you want to cry when your life is in turmoil, is evidence of your joy. Happiness is man-made, while joy is God-ordained. He created it and wanted us to have endless and unspeakable joy, meaning the joy we have cannot be indecisive, suppositious, or reproduced. The enemy cannot carbon copy that type of joy. We cannot live lifestyles incongruent with God's word and expect to have joy. He is the source of this sometimes confusing, often unfamiliar, and strangely peculiar type of joy. That type of joy also confuses the devil when he is fashioning objectives to work against you, creating symptoms of various forms in your life, and plotting to take you out, but you have the audacity to smile; it's inconceivable to the enemy. It's confusing and baffling for him, but continue to smile. Connected to the source, we can experience that beautiful, sublime, heavenly joy. Joy doesn't come from possessions and finances. Joy comes through our spirit being by faith. Our faith draws it in or attracts joy to us like a magnet. Financial wealth might bring happiness, but it will not bring you joy. And joy is long-lasting, not fleeting. As I see it, happiness is like a fugitive in this life. We have to keep chasing after it. Joy is not aloof to those who are connected to the source. Joy is connected to our spirit, and as long as our spirit stays connected to the source, our joy will remain. Joy brings restoration when happiness only brings ruination because it doesn't have the same endurance that joy transmits.

Joy is unremitting and unchanging, just like the source from which it comes. Our circumstances may be a recipient of our joy being full, meaning things might shift in our favor, but not the source of our joy being full. Our faith holds tightly to God's promises, and as we remain fervent in the word and press into our faith, that will establish our joy. Our faith has to be directed toward the God of love, who is able to fill us with joy. Psalm 90:14 (NLT) says, "Satisfy us each morning with your unfailing love, so we may sing for joy to the end of our lives." When we know that God loves us, we can be richly filled with joy. He is the one who satisfies us each morning with His unfailing love. Regardless of what we do, God still loves us. You see, joy has nothing to do with what we have or don't have nor what we do or don't do; it has a lot to do with God's love for us, our love for Him, and our willingness to give Him full reign over our lives. What is your response going to be to God's love? Based on His love toward us and our love for Him, we can have an interpersonal adventure in this earthly kingdom filled with amazing joy. We have to be receptive to and understand the vastness and depth of God's love for us. Don't believe me? Look through scripture for yourself to allow the scriptures to affirm God's love for you. Do not be deceived into thinking that joy and happiness are the same because they are definitely different. Even if used similarly, we need to understand the departure from what God created for us to what the enemy has tried to duplicate. Happiness is man-made and has nothing to do with God's love for us because it's not consistent nor rooted in our ardent faith in God and His love for us. If you know the difference, you won't be fooled, but the enemy is always looking to counterfeit what God has created. Our joy should remain no matter what is going on in the world because we know we have a deliverer who is coming to save us. His name is Jesus, Jewish by culture yet Christian by faith. Only He has the anointing to deliver us. Joy was freely given to us, yet most people don't know it. We didn't have to earn it or labor for it, as we do for happiness.

Joy was freely given to us, yet most Christ followers don't know it because they have been deceived or they haven't received fully from scripture what belongs to them. We didn't have to earn joy or work for it. In 1 Corinthians 2:12 (AMP), it says, "Now we have received, not the spirit of the world, but the [Holy] Spirit who is from God, so that we may know and understand the [wonderful] things freely given to us by God." We should be able to know and understand by the Holy Spirit who resides in us that joy is a free gift of God. We didn't have to buy it. We weren't expected to do anything for it apart from accepting the salvation gift of our Lord Jesus. I believe God wants all of us to have this joy. But it is expected for the Christ follower to experience godly joy on a regular basis in spite of earthly afflictions because we are experiencing it supernaturally—not from our sensory faculty but from the Spirit of God in us. We should be downloading it right from heaven into our heart since God is the source of abundant joy, and His spirit resides in us. If you back up a couple of scriptures in the same chapter, verse 11 tells us that for those who love God, there are benefits to be bestowed upon them. Joy is our benefit, while happiness is earned by circumstances. The difference is you have to work for it since it's not freely given. You must freely possess the joy that God has ordained and made a sacrifice for you to experience. It is powerful, a cousin to our faith, in that it can overlook the natural seeing into the spiritual realm of the end goal regardless of the situation. I see it this way: joy has a response of faith, and faith has a response of joy. Joy is beautiful, transmundane, and so magical it far exceeds happiness. Joy is your treasure to be cherished, just like your faith. It's not for the moment. It's for a lifetime. It is not earned but received. I encourage you to receive it freely.

Chapter 7

The Direction of Joy

The direction your life takes will determine the joy you have. Are you following God's direction for your life? His plan for you is the most important plan for you to follow. Or are you leading your life under your own direction? Persuaded by people, emotions, and evil forces to walk in ways contrary to God's word and your professed Christian faith? We cannot get upset with God when we are not following the plan He has for us. The direction of our joy always looks up, looks forward, and in the direction of the plan God has for our life. Our divination toward God's word and His affection for us enables the joy of God to flow to us as we move in the trajectory that He has for our lives. God has given us free will to choose the path we want to take; however, that path may not be the direction God has for us. It could be the path fraught with increased stress, adversity, frustration, and all things undesirable and deficient of the godly joy we are supposed to have. I personally would prefer not to look like I served two life sentences here on earth before being received in heaven. I want to make joy my guiding light before I see the King of Kings and the Lord of Lords. The joy we have is a mirror image of our relationship with God, living connected to Him or without Him. You cannot blame God for your poor choices when you don't follow His direction for your life. God doesn't want us walking through landmines and desert places. He also never intended for us to walk through this life alone. He would like for us to choose His wisdom, direction, and guidance since He knows the beginning from the end. We have to stay on a careful path, following God's lead and resisting the devil and evil forces even under temptation. Ephesians 5:15–16 (AMP) says,

"Therefore see that you walk carefully [living life with honor, purpose, and courage; shunning those who tolerate and enable evil], not as the unwise, but as wise [sensible, intelligent, discerning people], making the very most of your time [on earth, recognizing and taking advantage of each opportunity and using it with wisdom and diligence], because the days are [filled with] evil."

We have to live our lives walking carefully with honor, purpose, courage, and shunning all evil, as this scripture indicates, as this is the path God has for us. A path that is not void of wisdom as defined by this scripture. Proverbs tells us wisdom is the principal thing because, without it, mistakes will be made. The first part of this scripture is a description of what our Christian life should look like, subject to God's word on how He defines honor, purpose, courage, and shunning those who tolerate or enable evil. There are many biblical apologues that non-abstractly, allegorically, and metaphorically encapsulate honor, purpose, and courage. Honor is iconographic in Noah's life, visible in his relationship with God. He lived a life of honor and goodness while the whole world was engaging in corruption, but he was not. His behavior pleased the Lord, which led to him being chosen. Noah's honor was not hidden from God. As such, he was chosen to build the ark and was spared during the flood. The most honorable part of Noah's behavior is that he said yes to God's petition, deputizing himself to be mocked while building an ark when it had never rained in that region. Purpose can be witnessed in the life of Joseph, who found himself in a pit but knew that was not his final destination based upon the vision given by God. Later, he marvelously discovers himself in the palace, in a position serving parallel to Pharaoh. Joseph, one of the younger of his siblings, ends up being head over his older brothers, which was not the custom of ascendancy during that time. His brothers did bow to him, as evidenced in his vision. God was engineering some precedent-setting events, with Noah and Joseph as our examples. Then, there is the story of young David, the boy who defeats Goliath, not just in name but also in size. He didn't exude any fear. David wasn't even chosen but put himself forth to defend Judah against the Philistines. He had to disarm their defense, which was the giant who taunted them day and night. David demonstrated great courage in fighting to protect his kinsmen. There are also the stories of Moses, Esther, Gideon, Daniel, and so many others whose biblical accounts are examples of courage for us to follow. I am most impressed by the story of Gideon, who discounts himself before God, asks for two tangible signs that God is with him, never wavered in his trust toward God, then goes into battle with only 300 soldiers, winning against what seems to be a formidable Midian army with accompanying troops from neighboring tribes. It really is a dynamic story of courage and trust even as Gideon pursues the escaping kings to cut the neck off the snake. I would encourage you to read about each of these Bible stories. Even if you have read it once, do it again because a new revelation might come to you. Furthermore, Jesus is certainly an exemplary role model for us, demonstrating evidence for how we are to shun those who tolerate and enable evil as He did with the Pharisees and the Sadducees. He spoke out bravely yet lovingly when He discerned the perversion and wickedness in people's hearts. They were spiritually blind to what Jesus' transcendental mission would be, neglecting that the protecting cloak of God was with and upon Him. On multiple occasions, Jesus calls out their hypocrisy and wickedness as it did not reflect the true essence of God's Word. We can't walk in the direction of what seems right to us. The joy that we will manifest and should experience only appears when walking in the direction God has for us. Moreover, we have to operate in His wisdom. Jesus walked in the direction that God had ordained for His life, a direction that might have seemed joyless to the naked eye, but in the spirit, it was joyful.

The second part of the scripture above governs the administrative style of our walk. It should not lack wisdom, categorically defined as being sensible, intelligent, and discerning of people. We are also to take advantage of each opportunity with wisdom and diligence. The opportunities suggested here could be tests, not just something that has a semblance of fortune. We cannot appraise every test as something nullifying when, with wisdom and godly acumen, we can transform situations into opportunities. The direction of our joy also comes from viewing situations the way that God views them. God also stressed in His Word that He knows the plans and thoughts that He thinks toward us per Jeremiah 29:11 (AMP), "'For I know the plans and thoughts that I have for you,' says the Lord, 'plans for peace and well-being and not for disaster, to give you a future and a hope.'" His plans for us are not disastrous. He wants us to have hope and a good future; however, in order to have a personal account of all that God has promised us in His Word, we have to walk in accordance with the direction He has for us. I would surmise that if God is saying He has plans for peace and well-being, not for disaster, that is something for us to rejoice over. That is the framework for our joy. We can have joy in peace and in well-being. That is what God desires for us, even when tests and opportunities come our way. God's plan for us has not changed; however, He is looking for us to grow from each opportunity. He is looking for us to remain aligned with His Word and walk in the direction of His plans for us. He wants us to go through those tests with courage, knowing His plans for us are for peace and well-being, not disaster. His ultimate plan for us is for maturation through godly wisdom like Noah—we need to have a Noahic heart, especially during evil and corrupt times. Nobody ever matured by staying stagnant or never being challenged. Circumstances may come to test you, but stay the course in maintaining the direction God has for you. Challenge yourself to align your thoughts and plans with God so that you are going in the direction He has sculpted out for you before the foundation of the world. The direction of joy is through the voice of God. What we hear from Him is invaluable in influencing our thoughts and plans for our life. We can hear from God directly by being in His presence. The voice of the Holy Spirit, whom God provided in place of Jesus as a gift for us and our forever-abiding Comforter (John 14:16, 26–27), is always speaking. We can grieve the Holy Spirit by not waiting on, adhering to the voice of, and being influenced by His presence. As we stay immersed in the Word of God, we will hear the Holy Spirit minister to us, who is able to provide us with direction. Another way to hear the direction of the Holy Spirit is by praying in our heavenly language. Using my heavenly prayer language has been the most efficient and fastest way to hear the gentle, still voice of my heavenly Father.

Lastly, and likely most importantly, the text scripture above talks about "the days being filled with evil," which I believe we all can attest to and may have been affected by the evil happening in the world today. The evil in this world is not a surprise since it's prophesied in scripture, nor should it influence the direction of our joy. Remember, this evil that exists has a name behind it: it's the devil. We can't assume God is behind everything dreadful. That is such a misconception for us to believe. He wants bad things to happen to us, contrary to what His Word says, which doesn't sound right to me. God is not going to contradict His Word. He cannot lie. This is a devilish thought. It's a foreign thought that should be cast out. God is merciful. In the Old Testament, Jesus had not made His appearance in the flesh yet, and because the Israelites desired laws, God met their request (Exodus 19:8), and in the very next chapter (Chapter 20), God gives Moses the Ten Commandments, the New Covenant He now had with Israel. Yet, I emphasize that God answered their request, which is why we should be careful what we ask for, as it might not be what God intends for us. God never intended to give them laws to abide by...It's more custom and ritual. He was trying to free them from that dogma, but at their request, He granted it. This is why wisdom is needed in the midst of evil. However, prior to the laws, when Cain murdered Abel, God was merciful to Cain. He is not destroyed by God, but he was cursed to till the ground all the days of his life (Genesis 4:11–12), the consequence of his actions. God even demonstrated His mercy during the flood as the intention was to do away with evil so that the earth would yield forth good fruit, as in good people doing good things. I began to view this differently because it's not God's wrath. It's actually His favor so that mankind could live in a good world, which is still extended to us today because He has not destroyed the earth with a flood since then. Although evil does exist, that was His covenant promise to Noah. God's goal was to root out the evil, and it was a course correction for His people. Undoubtedly, that didn't last since God gave us free will. The will to choose good or evil. The Bible tells us the carnal mind, the flesh, is at enmity against God (Romans 8:7). I see this as a preventative measure so that we don't self-destruct, which could easily happen by doing things our own way. In the New Testament, Jesus is born for the redemption of our sins, so we are no longer under the Levitical laws but under God's grace. No more sin consciousness. Our covenant with God is shifted by the birth and brokenness of His Son, to which our reply to that atonement should be joyful praise. The sacrifice was made by both the Father and His Son. So, now, if we don't follow in His direction that

He has zealously laid out for us, He is not angry with us, nor is His desire for evil to befall us for all His people, Christ follower or not. God loves us. He loves you. That love emanates through the life of His Son. He still wants good for us in a joyful manner that only He can provide. Do not disregard the evil that is around you because God can use that to work toward your benefit as long as you are being directed by Him. This is the opportunity that we have in the goodness of God, although evil exists. We have to press into God's Word in spite of the evil today because our joy does not come from this world. It is found in the presence of God, His angels, following His precepts, staying in the Sabbath rest. It's also found in following after the fruits of the spirit, remaining connected to the vine, functioning from an Eden place, not burning out yet staying fueled and aflamed, and recognizing when troubles come our way that it's an opportunity for great joy.

Ever had a thought surface in your mind that seemed obstinate to God's Word? We have to stay aligned with God's thoughts and recognize when we have been derailed or taken a direction that is off course. To follow the direction of joy, you have to ask yourself what you are doing or not doing that is stealing your joy. You have to change directions when you get off course, but first, you must recognize you're off course. The Holy Spirit is that reservoir for communicating to us when we have deviated from the right direction. He is our compass for finding revived joy. Yet, without a relationship with the Holy Spirit, whom Jesus promised would be given to us as another Comforter, we cannot discern when we have pivoted in our direction. Notice Jesus said in John 14:16 that He will ask the Father, and He will give us, that giving is a gift. Since He gifted us with the Holy Spirit, He is not going to remove Him from us. Yet many of us have shelved the gift and wonder why our joy has depreciated. We have the responsibility of nurturing that relationship with the Holy Spirit. When we are attuned spiritually to our heavenly Father through the spirit, we will identify maladaptive patterns in our heart that are contrary to the direction God has for us in manifesting joy. Today, the fastest way to get off course is by listening to secular media and other sources about all the polarity and divisiveness in the world. How does listening to and meditating on that "nonsense" create joy for you? I think it's Satan's way of bombarding your mind so that you can slowly start thinking differently than how God has fashioned you to think or behave. He is stealthily and slowly trying to steal your joy. For example, one of those maladaptive and most talked about thoughts that the world is trying to feed us today is that there are skin color privileges. It's a deception of the enemy for those seeking joy to think they are unworthy of joy based on skin color. That's ridiculous and certainly a lie from the pit of hell. God never said in His Word that privilege is based on skin color. For those who are true Christ followers, we have Christian privilege, as noted in His Word. That Christian privilege overrules anything and everything. We should know that and believe it. As Christians, God has given us the same authority as Jesus and the same power that Jesus gave to the disciples. We are strong in the Lord and the power of His might. We have the ability and authority to manifest joy in our lives as we follow God's direction in the use of our faith. It has nothing to do with a manufactured lie made up by man. Your joy is not attached to your skin color; not even your happiness should be affiliated with that lie. We have to exercise our Christian privilege over this demonic prevarication that the enemy wants us all to believe that skin privilege outweighs Christian privilege—no way, devil. I am not buying it, and you shouldn't either. I have Christian privilege to obtain, create, produce, establish, and maintain joy that supersedes this earthly kingdom, which has nothing to do with skin color privileges. So the Bible teaches us that these negative thoughts are strongholds, per the NIV version of 2 Corinthians 10:4–5. But the Amplified Version tells us,

> *"The weapons of our warfare are not physical [weapons of flesh and blood]. Our weapons are divinely powerful for the destruction of fortresses. We are destroying sophisticated arguments and every exalted and proud thing that sets itself up against the [true] knowledge of God, and we are taking every thought and purpose captive to the obedience of Christ."*

We do not fight with carnal weapons while fighting spiritual battles. This negative thought process is a spiritual battle that the enemy is trying to manipulate us into believing. He is methodical about his deceptions and patient until we move toward believing something that is contrary to God's Word, and as we believe it, we will go in the direction of that belief. That lie begins to influence our thoughts; therefore, gradually, we begin to go in the direction of our most predominant thought, whether legitimate or a deception. If you want to attain God's unspeakable joy, then stop feeding on nonsense, which prevails on the direction of your joy. Junk influences our thoughts and doesn't feed our spirit. It pushes us further from the Spirit of God. Maintaining a thought process that is similar to God's thoughts will empower us to go in the direction God has laid out for us. We must give way to the voice of the Holy Spirit. We do have the mind of Christ (Philippians 2:5), so think like him, talk like him, behave like him. But to sustain that mind of Christ, we have to continue to replenish and renew our mind in the Word of God. We have to renew, meditate, feed on the Word of God daily. In one of the upcoming chapters, we will discuss the renewing of the mind in finding our joy.

God provides us direction through the Holy Spirit, not just on how to engage life but also on assessing our heart posture, renewing the mind, changing our thoughts, knowing our identity, and basically whatever we need. One of the roles of the Holy Spirit is to teach us all things (John 14:26b). As we change our thoughts and mind in relation to God's Word, we will follow the trajectory of our most prevalent and salient thought. Our thoughts need to be defined by the greatness in God's Word, and His Word should define us as our Creator. We need to know who we are in Christ. The direction of our joy is attached to our identity in Christ. The more we know Him in us, the more we become attracted to the Father who sent Him as a Redeemer for us. Our joy, like a magnet, is attracted to who God is in us. Is he a big God or a small God? That depends on how much you are using the Holy Spirit to connect to the Father. Remember, Jesus prayed to the Father that He would send us another Comforter who may abide with us forever. The Holy Spirit comes as an auxiliary to Jesus. Jesus paved the way. Likewise, the Holy Spirit helps us stay on the path when we give Him permission through relationship. What is your identity in relation to God? In the Bible, we are referred to as friends, co-workers, ambassadors, beloved, disciples, His children, sheep, the body of Christ, and the list of nouns and names goes on. We have a basic understanding of the definition of each term noted above, but we need to understand how it applies to us individually. Our identity is predicated on our understanding of our relationship to God. The direction of our joy comes from understanding what manner of spirit we have in us. The spirit in us determines whether we are walking toward joy. Remember, joy flows from the spirit because it's a spiritual process, not based on earthly matter. The spirit in us can be transposed based on our connection to God the Father, God the Son, and God the Holy Spirit. When our flesh begins to act up or be influenced by the carnality of this world, then we need to draw closer to God's Word to refine and redefine ourselves and reestablish our relationship to Him. This relationship will drive out any demonic spirits. Jesus even rebuked the disciples for not understanding the spirit that sent Him to them all. That can be found in Luke 9:51–56, which we will examine further in an upcoming chapter. It is important that God be at the nucleus of our spirit man. He created us. We did not evolve from monkeys. Our joy comes from Him, not the evolution of animals. The direction of our joy is contained in the spirit dwelling in us. That spirit is either of light or darkness, good or evil. You can receive the evidence of joy by changing your spirit. The Holy Spirit is on the road called joy. Draw on the Holy Spirit through whom we are expected to live our lives. The direction of your being has to have the right spirit attached to it that points you to the place of joy. God is the source of our joy, but the Holy Spirit helps us access it on earth. By following the Holy Spirit, we can all walk in the direction of joy that looks up and looks ahead.

Chapter 8

Actors in a Play

We are like actors in a play, those trying to strive for joy or others thriving with joy, and then there are the survivors. As actors, we all have a role, and whatever level our joy is at—striving, thriving, or surviving—we can distinguish the key players involved. Are you trying to obtain joy in your own might (striving), with God's help (thriving), or using the devil's tactics who try to camouflage happiness as joy (surviving)? When I continued thinking about this heavenly joy that God provided for us, I first had to realize that we all play a role in our joy; it's not just luck, an uncanny coincidence, or anything with secular meaning. The forces of good and evil have a role, just as we have the main role in acquiring heavenly joy. There are opportunities to smile every day and unlock that joy God authorized us to have, but we must figure out what actors we want in this play. That doesn't just include or exclude God and the devil, but also your peer group since the folks we socialize with have a great influence on our disposition. God has a part in my joy, the devil has a part in my joy, and yes, I play the biggest part in my joy—what I am doing and saying and what company I keep. Whether I have joy or not is largely based on what I am confessing, believing in, and mind-rehearsing daily since all of it reinforces my sadness or my joy. And who I am is what I most attract. Attracting joy is very much a demonstration of my disposition. The devil's role is to defraud and plagiarize our joy. He wants to take joy from us through various means, but more importantly, what he's done is disguise our happiness as joy. God's role in my joy was completed during the finished works of the cross. Let's focus on that part first.

There are two scriptures that come to mind regarding God's role in our joy: John 3:16 and 2 Peter 1:3. We have to recognize and honor God's role that it is finished. Our joy is complete because of what was done for us on behalf of His Son. To experience this heavenly joy, we have to understand it was innately God-given, and before we can engage the nine practices aforesaid, we have to accept Christ as our Savior because through that progression of faith is the mechanics of activating our joy. The first scripture is very familiar to many Christ followers, "For God so [greatly] loved and dearly prized the world, that he [even] gave His [One and} only begotten Son, so that whoever believes and trusts in Him [as Savior] shall not perish, but have eternal life" (John 3:16, AMP). The first part we have to notice in this scripture is "God so greatly loved." Sometimes, we neglect to meditate on that part of the scripture, but God loves us. The more we know that God loves us, the more accepting we are of the joy he has for us. Some folks might be feeling like they are not deserving of this heavenly joy for whatever reason: shame over behavior or thoughts, lies from the enemy, self-disdain, self-loathing, negative self-talk, but regardless of that, God loves us. Remind yourself daily that God loves you. He knew about the sin nature of man from the beginning, yet that didn't deter Him from giving His Son, which actually became the antecedent for why He gave His Son. Our impression of God will determine whether we believe we can experience the joy of God. If our impression of God is that He is not good and allows evil to happen, we may think that this heavenly joy is not prescribed to us or attainable for us. But in spite of what we have done or not done (accepting Christ as our Lord), He still loves us. You can repent from whatever it is you have done and just meditate on the fact that God loves you. Horrible things might have happened to you, but God still loves you. He did not authorize that evil to happen, although the devil will try to convince you of that lie. But once you realize how much God loves you, you will know that He wants you to have joy and happiness, but especially joy. The nine ways to discover your joy noted previously should be the standard for every Christ follower. You cannot have an image of God like your earthly parents or guardians because they are fallible. They have likely made mistakes intentionally or unintentionally and not expressed unconditional love toward you, but God does demonstrate unconditional love toward us all:

the just and the unjust. Our assumptions about God will influence how we experience His promises toward us, and joy is a promise. But our impression of God should be that He is good and He loves us. Not only did He love us, but that scripture in John says, "He gave." In giving of His Son, He literally gave us everything. The sacrifice was great, and so our joy can be great. It's full because of what He did through the willingness of His Son. We have so much to be thankful for because Jesus was willing, He knew what was to come, and though God did not remove this cup from Him, even in His sorrow, He was still willing. Tears come to my eyes thinking about this inexplicable and unthinkable peril that Jesus endured prior to and at the cross. He was put on trial for us to have all the promises in God's Word, and by accepting Him, we can have all these promises in our lives. God loves you, and He gave as an act of that love for you. That is the role He played. In 1 Peter 1:3 (KJV), we read that we have everything we need, "according as his divine power hath given unto us all things that pertain unto life and godliness, through the knowledge of him that hath called us to glory and virtue." This scripture only reinforces the finished works of the cross. This simply means we receive all things through knowledge from God. We must hold the vision of this fact that we have everything we need for living this life and living a whole life. Joy is from God and was given to us by Him in an effort to educate and reveal to us His goodness in this earthly kingdom. We would have no knowledge or conceptual impact of His goodness in this current kingdom without His heavenly joy. Not happiness but the joy that only God's provision has made for us. There is a classic song entitled "This Joy That I Have" that can remind us where our joy comes from. I can extract from the scripture in 1 Peter and through this vintage song that God's role in my joy is also that of the Creator. He is the Creator of our joy. And every role that God has in this play of our lives is finished! God has done all He plans to do for preparation of His heavenly joy toward us. When we choose heavenly joy, all the heavenly hosts of heaven, particularly our assigned angels, act on our behalf to call it into place. We have divine assistance ready to function for our benefit, imparting the favor of God in our lives and ready to transmit to us all the blessings God has for us. Joy can't be forced by your own effort to recognize it's an ecclesiastic act of God that has been completed at the cross. He is not going to do anything further, nor does He need to. You need to know it's been left to us, and the devil should have no part unless you give him access.

When I examine the role that the devil plays in our joy, it's one of corruption and demonic influence. He is the father of lies. The devil does not love you. He's actually jealous of all those who have been adopted into the kingdom of light. He wants to hijack our joy by constantly reminding us of our transgressions, our ineptness and inabilities, our sin nature, lies about what our personal narrative should be with God based on past experiences with our earthly father, and even trying to destroy our image of God as good. He is the enemy of our God-esteem and a fabricator of our self-image through our Maker. He wants to destroy us by using individual traumatic autobiographies to delude our belief about who God is in relation to us. Instead, wanting us to view God based on the imperfect experiences we have had with our earthly parents or guardians, not knowledgeable of the reality that our heavenly Father is different. He is transcendent from uncelestial beings, His compassion is transformative, and He is more loving towards us than we can ever comprehend. However, the devil's role was made clear in the beginning as the deceiver. In Genesis 3:1–5 (NLT), the devil's lies are evident to us as the deceiver. First, he asks the woman, known as Eve, after exiting the garden, "Did God really say you must not eat the fruit from any of the trees in the garden?" The serpent knew what God had said, and we know that because the scripture tells us he was the shrewdest of all the wild animals God had created. But his goal was one of conjecture, to play a guessing game or have her rethink what God had really said. He waits for her to respond, understanding he has the upper hand because now he has her in a place of second-guessing God. It's the same schemes he uses with us, trying to play on our weaknesses and ambiguities. When we don't trust what God has said, as the woman in the garden did, we give the enemy access. She understands that every tree is edible for them except the tree in the center of the garden, and if eaten, they will surely die. Then, the serpent lies again by saying, "You won't die!" after hearing the woman's response to his inquiry. The devil contradicts what God originally told Adam about the trees of the garden, who then passed it along to his wife. Think of it as a bad case of the telephone game. The woman tells the serpent about not eating and touching the tree of knowledge of good and evil, which Adam never even corrects her. God never said anything about touching the tree. Thankfully, we have the Holy Spirit for guidance and correction. Then, the serpent proceeds to tell the woman what he claims God doesn't want her to know, "God knows that your eyes will be opened as soon as you eat it, and you will be like God, knowing both good and evil." We have all probably learned that both the man and the woman were created in the image of God already per Genesis 1:27, so they were like God, but based on the deception by the serpent, they began to question their likeness to God followed by not knowing the image of God was in them. His deception is still present today, making us question the truth of God's word that He loves us. The question he poses now is, "Does God really love you if He allows XYZ to happen?" As a reminder, God is good, and there is a real devil that causes evil to happen and wants us to get angry with God or question what His Word says. It's part of his sardonic attack against us. The devil's role should not be hidden from us with regard to our joy. He wants to take it from us, as simple as that, and we have the authority and power not to give in to him. John 10:10 (KJV) provides a clearer description of the devil's role, "The thief cometh not but for to steal, and to kill, and to destroy; I am come that they might have life and that they might have it more abundantly." Our joy is a reflection of the abundant life. Do not let the enemy rob you or use your words or confessions to destroy you. Once our thought pattern shifts from one of peace to meditating on all the negative happening in our life or the world, that's when the devil is hoping discouragement will set in, so we begin speaking the negative we see, hear, or experience, and as we speak, we give him access to interfere with our joy. The first mistake the woman made in the garden was entertaining a conversation with the enemy. Do not entertain the enemy under any circumstances, as that is the first point of access. His role is to maliciously attack us. He's trying to silence and kill the Christ follower; he wants to destroy the plans of God and prevent us from experiencing heavenly joy, but I implore you not to be deceived, destroyed, or killed by the enemy because the greatest deception of all is assuming he doesn't exist. He is real and an opponent to us all who vow allegiance to Christ. He's after your joy and peace. You have a choice; don't surrender.

Our role as the main character in this play is to recognize the authority and power we have over our joy. Why? Because we decide whether to allow God the rights and access to our life for our joy to be fulfilled or whether the devil is given access and possession of our joy. If we are trying to obtain heavenly joy on our own, we will never be successful. Our joy comes through covenant with God, by accepting Jesus as Lord over lives since nobody can come to God except through His Son. We have access to the promise of joy through covenant. It's where God operates with omnipotent influence. Joy was already given to us once we rededicate our lives back to Christ. We have to accept it and not give it up to the evil one or any demonic force in this earthly kingdom. In 2 Corinthians 5:17 (KJV), we are given instructions on our Christ walk, "Therefore if any man be in Christ, he is a new creature: old things are passed away; behold, all things are become new." So, if we are Christ followers, the instruction is that we are supposed to be new creatures; the past is no longer relevant, and we are now new. If new, then we should be thinking like Christ, talking like Christ, and acting like Christ. I am certainly guilty of not doing the aforesaid all the time. I have double-dipped living as a new creation in Christ, but not always thinking, talking, and acting like Christ. We all do it, but we are supposed to be different. We are supposed to be new now, not operating under the old way of doing things. Being new creatures gives us access to the promises of God housed in the supernatural realm by using our God-like faith. Joy is found in the supernatural things of God, but we have to claim those things by faith. What are those things being claimed by faith? Peace, purpose, wisdom, healing, prosperity, and so forth. You can claim faith, but if there is no evidence of your faith from the supernatural to the natural, then there is a problem, and the problem is not God. The Bible tells us in James 2:26 that faith without works is dead, and so our preparation and practice is a byproduct of this faith walk. Our joy shows up sometimes more in the supernatural, especially when kindled by faith, but it should be evidenced in the natural, channeled from a place of faith as new creatures in Christ. You must understand our faith is the carrier. Men should have Abraham or Elisha-like faith. Women should have Hannah or Deborah-like faith. Additionally, there are many others in the Bible where we could emulate their faith walk. They had supernatural faith and did not consider anything contrary to God's Word or what they could experience through their five senses but maintained faith and trust in God. So, one of the roles we have to play in our joy walk is recognizing we are new creatures and thus have access to the promises of God and the supernatural things of God using our God-like faith. We don't have to feel joyful to know joy is present in our lives because it's not about the senses: olfactory, gustatory, auditory, visual, or tactile. The unseen things are eternal per 2 Corinthians 4:18, and that's where we should focus our attention. It's about what God's word says to us and do we trust God's word. Secondly, our role is to resist the devil. Don't be like the woman in the garden as she entertained what the enemy said. Stop listening to him, renew your mind in the Word, and speak up when he speaks to you. The Bible prods us about this very point, James 4:7 (AMP), "So submit to [the authority of] God. Resist the devil [stand firm against him] and he will flee from you." The Message translation tells us to "yell a loud no to the devil and watch him make himself scarce." That is the talking back we all need to do so that we never give the devil any opportunity to even put a lie in our minds. I know some of us were taught never to talk back, but when it comes to the devil, you have a right to talk back and refuse anything he tries to exploit to you. He has been a liar from the beginning and will always be a liar. Another role we have is also to stay in the mode of learning. We may not understand everything that is happening to us or in this world, and circumstances might arise that create impulsive reactions, cerebral responses, or distressing triggers. In the wake of all these emotions, maybe we should ask ourselves what we can learn from these circumstances instead of, "God, remove this cup from me" (Luke 22:42). Certainly, what we go through cannot be likened to what our precious Jesus went through after being arrested by a band of accusatory men and officers doing the work of the chief priests and Pharisees, alleging Jesus committed blasphemy and apostasy against the church. Isaiah, the book of the Bible that most closely references Jesus, the Messiah, notably talks about Jesus' body being marred and the flesh falling off of Him, disfigured to the point where He barely looked recognizable as a human. I am not talking about abuse. I am specifically speaking to situations and circumstances that are oppressive and, yes, hard to manage, but not necessarily akin to what Jesus went through. Every novel situation invites an opportunity for learning and growth, and should we decide to take that position, it can yield more positive prospects than negative. Lastly, our role includes preparing our hearts and our mouth for joy. It's almost impossible to receive joy when the exchange of discouraging words and a bitter heart impedes joy from passing through to you. Complaining, discouraging, and invalidating words reinforce bitterness in the heart. As I have often said during sessions, you cannot get better by being bitter. We have to transform our words if we want to heal our hearts. The Bible compares pleasant words to honeycomb, indicating they are sweet and delightful to the soul (mind, emotions, will, intellect) and healing to the bones as in the body (Proverbs 16:24). Pay close attention to the words sweet and delightful, sweet meaning pleasing to the taste and induced by sugars, agreeable or gratifying, marked by gentle good humor or kindliness as defined by Merriam-Webster Dictionary. "Delightful," taken from the root word "delight," also means "joy," as we discovered previously and used interchangeably throughout scripture. As we conceptualize this further, agreeable, gratifying, good-humored, kind, and joyful words are good for our mind, emotions, will, and intellect that compromise the soul. To further amplify this point, let's look at a few scriptures, the first being in Proverbs 12:25 (KJV), "Heaviness in the heart of man maketh it stoop: but a good word maketh it glad." What does this really mean? Looking at various translations, I could see that the heaviness referred to is anxiety, worry, fear, depression, all things disavowing and oppressive to our heart, including bitterness. These things weigh the heart down, and it stoops. However, hearing good words from the gospel can make our heart full of joy. This tells me that we have to get in the Word and let it penetrate our heart. Proverbs 14:10 (NIV) states, "Each heart knows its own bitterness, and no one else can share its joy." No one else understands or fully knows the bitterness in a person's heart because they are not privy to that person's experiences, and if so, they still do not comprehend the impact. The pain in the heart of a person is subjective. Bitterness in the heart is grief, and it's held there covertly until eradicated, but only God judges the heart, so He knows what we are holding there, and only He can help us heal it. No one can experience the joy of anyone with a bitter heart. They might be laughing outwardly but still hurting inwardly. We have to examine our own hearts to determine what bitterness is being held there and look to scripture for how to heal. The aforesaid scripture doesn't give us a remedy. It only makes a statement about bitterness in the heart. The solution can be found in Proverbs 16:1–3,

> *"The plans and reflections of the heart belong to man, But the [wise] answer of the tongue is from the Lord. All the ways of a man are clean and innocent in his own eyes [and he may see nothing wrong with his actions], But the Lord weighs and examines the motives and intents [of the heart and knows the truth]. Commit your works to the Lord [submit and trust them to Him], And your plans will succeed [if you respond to His will and guidance]."*

We have to speak wise words from the Lord to ourselves to change our heart posture because what we plan and reflect on in the heart, bitter or brilliant, belongs to us, not God. We may think our actions are demonstrating joy and kindness, but God knows the heart. If we commit our actions to Him, then our plans will be successful and not backfire. Speak wise words and commit your actions to the Lord. Don't look at circumstances and the evil around you. Then, your words will be His words, delightful, and your heart will be healed. Joy is magnetic and contagious. If you want more of it, you have to draw it in. Proverbs 15:13 (KJV) reminds us, "A merry heart maketh a cheerful countenance: but by sorrow of the heart the spirit is broken." As the primary actor in our joy, we have to keep a cheerful heart and be mindful of what we say as it reinforces the reflections of the heart.

Chapter 9

For the Joy Set Before Him...He Endured the Cross

We have all likely read or heard this scripture in Hebrews 12:2 (NIV), "Fixing our eyes on Jesus, the pioneer and perfecter of faith. For the joy set before him he endured the cross, scorning its shame, and sat down at the right hand of the throne of God," but do we fully understand the sacrifice Jesus made for us? The joy He held was wrapped up in enduring the pain of the cross, an oppressive death, a suffering that we would never know or have to experience because Jesus took our place to be scorned and humiliated. But because Jesus knew the goal at the end of His suffering was so great to endure on our behalf, and yet He did it anyway. The Amplified Bible points to the direction of His joy at "accomplishing the goal." He endured the humiliation of the cross to take on the disease of sin so that we could have a place again with the Father. Let's go back to the beginning before the cross. Jesus predicts His own death and prophesies about this to the disciples on multiple occasions to prepare them for the transition. The final prophetic word of His death can be found in Matthew 26:2 (KJV), "Ye know that after two days is the feast of the Passover, and the Son of man is betrayed to be crucified." It's clear that Jesus must have learned this from the Father, as the Bible tells us in John 14:10 that the words He spoke are from the Father. God provided Him with knowledge of the day and hour of His death, which I view as merciful. However, we know He doesn't know the hour of His return per Matthew 24:36. Jesus knew what His sacrifice would be accomplishing, which was more important in His death than in His second coming. His death, burial, and resurrection were important to Him because of what they accomplished for us. Jesus didn't die on the cross to be a hero for Himself but as a settlement for our transgressions against the Father. We essentially committed treason against our Creator, and that trespass was too grandiose for the exchange not to be equally grandiose. Jesus was a gift, almost like a dowry, meant to bring us back in right standing with the bridegroom, our Father.

Before I understood what the cross perfectly represented being a new pupil in Christ some thirty years ago, I had numerous questions about why Jesus was betrayed. For a long time, I found myself reading scriptures about Jesus' anticipated death and those who betrayed Him as they were envious of the knowledge He obtained and the teachings He shared without a conventional education, which made me somewhat angry. Why would they persecute a man who came in peace to save us from our sins? First, we have to look at the early church and Christian life at that time. The supremacy of Christ in the early church was shrouded by suspicion, political autocracy, and rejection. Spreading the gospel of Christ during those times was often met with strong animosity and staunch adversity partly because of the polarity of the Jewish faith and idolatry worship, along with other religious sects and false prophets appearing. And clearly, there were false prophets present because Jesus even cautions about believing and following after false profits which come in sheep's clothing but could be devouring wolves (Matthew 7:15) and warns about it again during the future age of the church in Matthew 24:24. Jesus, Himself, was viewed as a false prophet by the Pharisees and Sadducees because they came to test Him (Matthew 16:1, and John 7:45–47), the motive being unbelief. They wanted to see a miracle from Him investigating His claim as a true prophet from the God of Israel. In Matthew 21:23, the chief priests were questioning Jesus' authority, another indication of their incredulity of His teachings. Caiaphas, the high priest, basically disliked how Jesus was being idolized. They all continued to falsely claim that Jesus was not the Messiah nor sent by God and spoke contrary to His teachings. The animus toward the Christian faith also may have had a lot to do with the novelty of it, as people tend to reject the contemporary and unfashionable. The church then had members who strictly adhered to the Jewish customs and teachings but lost sight of God as it became more ritualistic as opposed to relationship-centered and fellowship-oriented. Then there was the Roman polytheistic empire that rejected the spread of Christianity as it was in stout conflict with their ideological beliefs and paganistic practices borrowed from ancient Grecian rituals. We have all likely read or learned about the Greek gods of their time, such as Zeus, Apollo, Athena, Aphrodite, and Poseidon. I certainly did while learning about Greek mythology in school, and the aforesaid were the great names that always came to mind. It was common to make these dogmatic pagan practices to the deities of emperors, exalting them above the One True God, and not only for the Romans but some exiled Jews who also gave in to these atheistic practices. Worshiping these shrines and cultic practices has been happening for ages. It's revealed in the Old Testament that even the Egyptians believed in gods and goddesses and continued to do so throughout time. Examples include building the tower of Babel and the Israelites creating a golden image for adoration while in the wilderness. In Egypt, the Israelites were trying to practice their faith among people who didn't adopt similar dogma, and such was the case during the time of Jesus among the Romans and is certainly present today. There were many who were spiritually blind and thus couldn't see the vision of what Christ represented. I still couldn't understand, though, for the longest why they could not see that Jesus was the Son of God, born to give us eternal life with the Father. Instead, they despised His teachings and considered them too hard to hear (John 6:60), consequentially making accusations of treason against Jesus and His disciples. It wasn't until I matured, not chronologically, but in the things of the Word of God, that I understood there had to be an antagonist in this Bible story in order for the prophesies to be fulfilled. You know...you recall studying the protagonist and antagonist from literary novels in English class. There is at least one good guy and one bad guy, a villain and a hero in every story. That's when I came to wholly understand why there had to be an antagonist in these non-fictional events of the Bible, sitting in sixth-grade English class, comprehending the legendary characters and conflict of folklore. The protagonists in this non-fiction story were Jesus and possibly His disciples, who didn't fully understand the reason for Jesus' death. They sit with Him at the Passover meal while He discloses to them again what is about to happen before going to the Garden of Gethsemane, essentially the scene of the indictment, where Jesus is eventually betrayed by

Judas with a kiss. Why a kiss? It was not just a symbol of betrayal but a sweet yet bitter way to give Jesus over to the agents of the enemy. Jesus is made a mockery of as part of the public humiliation He had to experience. The chief priests, scribes, and elders of the church also mocked the Son of Man, questioning His doctrine, His disciples, and even hitting Him for how He spoke following His arrest (John 18:19–24). And actually, before the cross, He was mocked by the governor's soldiers. He was stripped nude, placed in a scarlet robe, like the branding of a scarlet letter, and a thorn crown placed upon His head. They kneeled and bowed before Him, saying, "Hail King of the Jews," spitting on Him, striking Him, and laughing (Matthew 27:29–30). They mock Him again while on the cross, yelling for Him to save Himself as He saved others and come down off the cross (Matthew 27:41–43). They are tempting Him with a small reward to save Himself, but the bigger reward awaited, to glorify the Father, not Himself, and be the liberator from our sin-bound nature. Did He have the jurisdiction to take Himself off the cross? Of course, He did. He had the dominion to do it. A legion of angels would have come to save Him prior to the cross if that was the intended plan. However, it was not God's will as Jesus asked in the Garden of Gethsemane, "If it be thy will, remove this cup from me." It was clearly not God's will. God knew what had to be done, and Jesus was willing to make the sacrifice. Jesus was a willing participant, and even understanding the worst to come, He surrendered to the Father's plan, unlike the animal sacrifices under the Old Covenant, as they were sacrificial lambs without any personal election to do so. Jesus is pronounced dead by the piercing of His side, removed from the cross, buried in a tomb with a guard set before the door. No man could have removed Jesus from the tomb except the Almighty God. I was always glad that a guard was set before the tomb because then Jesus being raised from the dead by God could not be done in human strength, and the Almighty could not be denied.

Jesus was tempted in many ways, and every way possible according to the Bible, and even at the cross, as was previously mentioned, but He refused to give in. The serpent, under the direction of the devil, tempted the woman in the Garden of Eden to eat of the fruit, trying to entice her with a smaller, insignificant reward. We all know the woman and Adam were like God, as many have taught on the subject, and the Bible explains they had an image of their Creator in them because they were made by the Creator, God Himself. However, they were tempted and enticed for a reward with no visible profit, unlike Jesus, who was tempted in every way even before the cross and chose not to give in to temptation. What was the difference? I believe Jesus, also the image of God, saw the bigger picture. He understood what was at stake as opposed to Adam, who didn't spiritually see the bigger picture God had set before him. Jesus saw the greater reward that God the Father would raise Him from the dead in three days as Jesus also prophesied to His disciples, then sent Him to them to see His resurrection, and is now seated at the right hand of the Father, the place of authority to be a go-between for us and God. We can praise God for not just sending His Son but for the joy that was set before Jesus. He endured the cross for the sake of those He loved despite His ability to remove Himself from the cross. Jesus could have told the Father, "No, thank you," as Adam denied and defied His Creator. He didn't give in to the temptation, seeking immediate gratification to save Himself because the most important aspect of this sacrifice was that Jesus saved us publicly as He was crucified publicly. His death could not be denied, and subsequently, He was raised from mortality to immortality and seen publicly so that His prophecy of rebirth could give light to the authority in God's Word. Mankind cannot deny His death or resurrection, although they still try to, but because Adam's fall was so public [Adam's fall is publicized in Bibles everywhere and reflected in the earth], Jesus' redemption had to be equally publicized, including the unimaginable harshness He endured. The revilement that Jesus suffered and the temptation that He endured serve as a lesson to all Christ followers on how to lead our lives. Jesus didn't have an identity crisis or a crisis of kingdoms. He knew what was expected of Him and chose the kingdom He would serve, preceding the foundation of this world. He was here for one purpose: establishing the kingdom of God here on earth. He did that through teaching directly—the sermon on the mount is one example—and indirectly through His actions, as evidenced by the miracles He did: healing the leper in Matthew 8:1–4 and making water into wine in John 2:1–11. The goal of the naysayers was to imprison or exterminate the kingdom message, but even that could not be hampered based on the move of God. The opposers thought that by killing the representative, they could kill the message, yet that still was not the answer. But by putting Jesus to death, they actually made Him a martyr and the model example for many of His disciples to follow even after His physical death. The joy set before Jesus was to be the mediator of our sins to the Father. Our sins required public compensation by Jesus since our sins came from a public fall by Adam. Jesus brokered a better deal between us and the Father. As the arbitrator of a better covenant, we can have eternal joy because we are not lost but now under grace.

Chapter 10

The Joy That Shares

We have the joy of reconciliation with God because of our Lord Jesus Christ (the Messiah, the Anointed One) per Romans 5:1 (AMP). And so the etiology of the heavenly joy we have did not manifest by our own doing. We didn't do anything to earn it because this joy was predestined by God for us. Most importantly, recognize that the joy given to you by God is not for you alone. It is supposed to be shared. The Bible tells me that joy was first shared with us through the Godhead, God the Father, God through His Son, and now the Holy Spirit. Ecclesiastes 2:26 (KJV) states,

> *"For God giveth to a man that is good in his sight wisdom, and knowledge, and joy: but to the sinner he giveth travail, to gather and to heap up, that he may give to him that is good before God. This also is vanity and vexation of the spirit."*

Now, if God is able to give us wisdom, knowledge, and joy, then He must have it to give. We can't give what we don't have ourselves. God is giving us what He has, His joy, so it's heavenly joy, to those who are good in His sight, so He assesses our goodness, but He also has the authority to give travail to the sinner. Joy may be the first introduction that the dead in Christ need to become alive in their spirit and become acquainted with the joy of God. Another scripture demonstrates that joy is passed to us from the trinity of God, and it comes from John 17:13 (NLT), "Now I am coming to you. I told them many things while I was with them in this world so they would be filled with my joy." Jesus takes ownership of this joy while praying to the Father before He is to be arrested. He ministered to us through the Word of God as a way to translate and transfer His joy to us. Joy belongs to the Godhead and was shared with us so we, as the light in this world, could share it with others. Jesus sacrificed His life so that all of us in this world could rejoice at the fulfillment of prophecy and at our Lord's return. He is coming again to us who believe, and we will have joy that no man can take (John 16:20–22). We have become conjoined to the joy gift that was God-given from the beginning because we believed.

Not only should we share our joy because it was first shared with us as the light in the world, but also for the purpose of restocking. The easiest way to continue replenishing our joy is by sharing it because, in the act of sharing, we receive abundantly more to give. The same principle is operative here as it is for monetary giving,

> *"Give, and you will receive. Your gift will return to you in full—pressed down, shaken together to make room for more, running over, and poured into your lap. The amount you give will determine the amount you get back."*
>
> Luke 6:38 (NLT)

If you want more joy, then give more joy, sow it as a seed, and you can sow it simply in a smile. Many people are hurting today, and just by sowing a smile, we can lift a person's spirit, make their heart smile, and even give them encouragement. Joy is a heavenly gift from God, but not just for us alone. It is to be shared with others around us so that they can heal, grow, and hopefully find joy themselves through their relationship with God and faith in His Word. We can sow joy in many ways. A smile is the least of these, but giving your time in ministry, alms, or other humane services through acts of kindnesses and deeds that glorify God, such as showing love and forgiveness to the person who cut you off on the road or the store clerk who seems annoyed with you asking a question or your boss who you feel might be targeting you or shaking a hand or giving a hug, which might take a little more effort are other ways to demonstrate joy. My favorite, greetings of joy—how about a good morning to the person taking your order at Dunkin Donuts or a good afternoon to the person at Burger King or wherever you go to eat? These are seeds of good tidings being sown in joy. Instead of just putting in an order, we need to greet those who are taking care of us...sow some seeds of joy. Through altruistic acts, we can express joy to others as well. It doesn't take wealth to be altruistic—the deeds of generosity can be shown in many ways, as aforementioned. Though there are so many more practices of benevolence, you just simply do what God puts on your heart to do. Some acts of benevolence may include sharing hope with someone who feels hopeless, helping someone pursue their dreams through earnest, compassionate fellowship, offering sympathy to the grieving, showing clemency in the face of differences. I am often reminded of the scripture in Proverbs 18:24a, "A man that hath friends must shew himself friendly." As Christ followers, we have to show ourselves to be friendly and not just in church. We can do so by sharing the joy provisioned to us by our matrimony with Christ. Others may not share in that same union, but we have the benefit of it, and some may only know by us.

This heavenly joy becomes stirred up as we share it. Recall when you first received something that made you excited, such as getting your first car, getting your degree, or getting saved, and you wanted to share it with everyone and show it off. The joy we have from God is meant to be shared. This might be the only time it's acceptable to engage in grandstanding behaviors when it comes to the things of God: our salvation, our faith, our heavenly joy. Our sharing can be restorative for us and others. It's a way for us to receive God's peace and to pass that peace along. It's an act of staying connected to Jesus by finishing the work He started. It's an avenue for ensuring our joy doesn't become vulnerable or suppressed. Joy sharing is an expression of hope, a renewal to our soul, and an intentional appreciation of goodness. Think about how you can share joy with others and what that would look like for you. As you practice joy, ponder the influence that you have on others, how it impacts your attitude, and in what way you are being stirred up.

Chapter 11

The Road Called Joy

You can use all nine of these pathways to find joy and still say to yourself, "Where is the joy God has for me? Why is it not present in my life? Is it truly not present?" Or are you not walking on the right path? Joy is not only an attitude you create, a posture you take, but also a road you make that continues to have a front-facing position. The path to joy is a path that lies in front of you, not behind. You have to let go of the past, the mistakes you made, the hurt that came with it, the bitterness and anger, and you have to move forward to the future that's right in front of you. Joy is a road in the future. Joy looks and stays focused on God's word. Joy keeps truth in its sight. The name of that road is called the Joy Road. One of the things we have to decide is whether we want to experience this heavenly joy in our life. You have to choose it, and then you have to walk on the path where joy lives. You have to keep joy as your vision. Yes, I can do all nine of these scriptures and find that there's no joy in my life if I'm looking at it as just a formula and not choosing joy. It is not a chore. It's a choice. Taking the position of "every day invites joy for me because of who I know, not based upon how I feel or the circumstances that surround me" is a posture of victory on this road called Joy. Receiving your God-given joy is a combination of conditions using the scriptures above, making a conscious choice, and shifting your mindset. But you have to make that choice, not someone else, not a family member, not even God, only you. You choose to have joy in your life. God has given us that as one of His many blessings. It's a benefit to us, but we still have to choose it. Someone can offer you a gift, but you have to choose to receive it. God has offered us many gifts that some Christ followers are not choosing to receive. It's like prosperity; God desires that we be prosperous so that we can also participate in the kingdom of God monetarily, but it's a road that you have to choose. You have to choose to do something different than what you're doing right now. You have to listen to the voice of the Holy Spirit as He gives you marvelous ideas that are prosperity-driven ideas. You have to choose that you're tired of living like a pauper. Once you make that choice, then angels come alongside you, and so does the Holy Spirit, to help move you in the direction of prosperity. Or, like healing, someone can lay their hands on you, but you have to choose to receive the anointing to be healed. It's no different from prosperity. It's the same with healing. You have to choose to be well. Do not choose your symptoms. If you put too much faith in your symptoms instead of God's Word, you will not be healed. It's a choice. Joy works the same way. When you make that choice, the heavenly host of angels, along with the Holy Spirit, come right alongside you to make sure that joy shows up in your life. So, what lies down the Joy Road? It's everything that God said that the Christ follower can have in His Word. All those things that make you joyous, all those things that make you want to jump up and down, all those things that put a smile on your face, all those things that give you a feeling of elation, those are the things that create joy. And for more details on what lies down the Joy Road, I suggest reading your Bible. That's right, joy is found in God's Word. Period, said it, and done. Joy can be right at your fingertips. You have to make that decision. You have to choose joy and remain consistent with that choice, and then trust God's Word. You have to choose to do the scriptures aforesaid to follow through with them daily, and you have to choose the road called Joy. Someone might say that's way too simple. It's not as simple as you might think. The enemy is trying to set booby traps to create a joyless life, so when negative circumstances come up, outcomes aren't as you expected, or everything seems to be going wrong, that's when you are tested to make the choice to maintain joy in the face of afflictions. It might be tough to do if you have not preset your mind to choose the road called Joy. I strongly suggest choosing the road called Joy in advance of anything happening, and then just keep your mind set on it. For those who believe they have chosen joy and are still not aware of its presence, I would suggest re-examining if your actions and attitude reflect the choice you made. You can't make the choice without shifting your actions and attitude. There has to be symmetry and consistency. You have to equally hold tightly to your choice while maintaining the actions and attitude of joy. You have to choose joy without toggling back and forth with joylessness. You have to assert your decision to yourself yet also make that position clear to the devil. You have to demonstrate corresponding action along with the choice made. If you are choosing the road called Joy, take more opportunities to smile, particularly in the face of opposition. In terms of your attitude, take a posture and position of faith. Make a vow to yourself not to move from that disposition of faith until you notice the presence of joy in your life. These are just a few examples of your actions and attitude reflective of your choice to choose joy, but certainly more exist that you can come up with on your own. Make a choice and ensure your actions and attitude align with that choice. Maybe even saying it aloud, "I choose joy," when you aren't seeing or feeling it. You don't necessarily have to see or feel it anyway. It's a philosophy and a way of life. You have to keep saying it until you draw it in and receive it in your spirit. Go on. I challenge you to do it right now, in the moment, yell it out, and make the devil angry. "Joy is mine. I choose the road called Joy." Say it with conviction, amplifying a voice of faith instead of fear. Joy doesn't exemplify fear. It exposes our faith. The evidence of your joy is actually being able to stay in a place of faith. Make a choice, stick with it, and don't be moved...choose the road called Joy.

Chapter 12

The Mind-Cleansing Steps of Joy

I have touched on the preponderance of renewing our mind at certain points throughout the book, but I want to reveal more in-depth why that is such a necessity. Many books have been written about this very subject. Even in that fact, it demonstrates the value this topic holds for the true believer. We need to hear it often because even the most erudite person is forgetful. It is critical for us to understand that the enemy cannot directly affect our spirit. He has not been given access to it, nor does he have the authority, so where he tries to create upset is in our soul, where our mind, emotions, will, and intellect are housed. The hellish attacks on the soul then begin to impact the body, resulting in psychosomatic complaints. If the devil's infection stays in the soul long enough, it can create psychological complaints. This is not satirical. It is real. The devil is after our soul, specifically the Christ follower, because he can't have our spirit. He wants to attack our peace and does it through our mind. The devil tries to inject the spirit of fear into our thought life. Fear will hold you back from fully receiving the joy that Jesus died for us to receive and God promised. This is a spiritual attack and has to be addressed in the spirit by renewing the mind. We have mentioned our bedrock scripture previously for this principle from Romans 12:2 (KJV), "And be not conformed to this world: but be ye transformed by the renewing of your mind, that ye may prove what is that good, and acceptable, and perfect, will of God." Why do it? Because we are programmed to stay focused on negativity as a pain avoider and mechanism for safety. Maintaining those negative experiences becomes a natural prophylactic and protection against harm. It's our animal instinct to avoid adversity and afflictions, which is why we have to renew the mind. How do we renew the mind? There isn't one clear method for doing so. There are multiple methods for transformation to happen in our minds and thoughts. We will look at various ways to achieve this renewing process through actual scripture. But before we get there, I want to describe how I think of renewing the mind. As I see it, it is the process of repeatedly hearing the Word, meditating on the Word, writing the Word, psalms of the Word, and flooding ourselves with the Word. The Word is the Bible and our key to unlocking the cleansing steps of joy with this transformation process. It's a radical change that takes place. The first step to renewing the mind can be the simple task of taking note of what you are thinking about. My pastor provided us with a handout one Sunday that is an outstanding resource for testing your thoughts against the Word to make sure they align. Testing your thoughts against the Word is important for two main reasons: (1) as a Christ follower, our thoughts should align with God's thoughts, and (2) the Word is the truth and no lie. We have to base our thoughts on the truth in God's Word, not the disharmony on this earth, since there is no joy in the latter. Pastor Chris Caton's the Thinking Test might be a great place for you to start (a copy has been included in the rear of the book). This test is based on the scripture in Philippians 4:6–9, and filtering your thoughts through those sets of scriptures is a good way to determine what you are thinking about. The renewed mind doesn't think on fear, worry, sadness, depression, or the like. The renewed mind is disciplined, so it goes back to judge itself against the Word, and the Word becomes a boundary for our mind. Please do not be alarmed if you find your thoughts are not aligned with the Word of God, particularly while taking the Thinking Test. You still have the authority to change that by locating scriptures that shift your mind back to where it should be, dependent on your thought matter. Then, medicate your thoughts with meditation on those scriptures until they synchronize with your spirit, similar to medicating your body with pharmaceutical drugs as prescribed by your doctor. God's prescription for us is uncomplicated, has no side effects or shelf life, and involves renewing the mind day after day. If the mind won't yield up its negative thoughts, then take charge through communion and consecration to our Lord as another way to transform yourself. Communion is the process of taking the sacraments, but I am not only referring to that sacred ceremony, communing or communion with God, but also spending time with Him. Consecration is the sanctification of our body back to Him through fasting. You can consecrate your body to shift your thoughts back in to right standing with God's thoughts. As you fast, you give less attention to and lose interest in things that are not God-driven. As a reminder, man does not live by bread alone but by words, and not just any words—godly words. Thus, you can substitute feeding your body for feeding your spirit. The work of changing our thoughts in the mind is done by staying in the presence of God and in the Word. So, why do we need to renew our mind? Cleansing the mind is our immunity from secular chaos and the most compassionate thing we can do for ourselves besides our salvation. Without carefully engaging this step, we would never be able to cleanse ourselves from all the debris that swamps and impacts our hearts, thoughts, and attitudes as a result of living in this fallen world. It can harden the heart, create cynical thoughts, and produce an attitude obstinate to God. That debris is an avalanche that will cause you to lose your mind and have you thinking you are mentally unstable or you have lost the fight. It can also cost us our joy if we give it focus. The bottom line is that mankind is not perfect, and we all have sinned and fallen short of the glory of God; thus, we live in a world with imperfect and fallen people.

> *"This righteousness of God comes through faith in Jesus Christ for all those [Jew or Gentile] who believe [and trust in Him and acknowledge Him as God's Son]. There is no distinction, since all have sinned and continually fall short of the glory of God."*
>
> Romans 3:22–23 (AMP)

We only become righteous through the acceptance of Jesus, and until the world does that, acknowledge and accept Jesus as Lord, then we will never live in a perfect world. The latter part of this scripture indicates that we have sinned and continually fall short; we make mistakes over and over again, but thankfully, God's grace is sufficient for us. His grace is a cloak for our sins. Mankind is not infallible. We cannot expect to get good out of a world that is broken and under the veil of sin. Sometimes, living in this world can be beyond overwhelming for some people, as they let themselves be influenced and troubled by what is going on in this earthly kingdom. We have to know that this world contains both believers and non-believers. Some non-believers are on assignment from the devil, just as some believers and Christ followers are on assignment from God, to hinder and be a barrier to us exercising our faith, attaining the promises of God, and testing our spiritual fruits. As we understand this fact, we don't have to be in disbelief when bad things happen. We can discern the spirit at work, whether it be godly or devilish. The world is chaotic, truculent, acrimonious, and malevolent, yet through all the clouds, fog, debris, and craziness, there is some good that exists in the washing of our iniquities through the blood of the lamb. That lamb is Jesus. That and only that is what makes us good and righteous before God. It helps us maintain strength during challenging times and walk in the good we want to see in this world. The lamb of Jesus Christ has cleansing power, and it can purify our minds from the hardness of this world. Our joy was a promise from God, but you better believe the enemy is not going to make it easy for us to hold onto it.

Jesus' death and subsequent resurrection have licensed us to walk in that covenant joy God promised in His Word. Staying conformed to this world holds us back from being transformed in our faith and attaining the God kind of joy we should have. I am not saying the world is evil. The Bible says it. First John 5:20 (NLT) states, "We know that we are children of God and that the world around us is under the control of the evil one." The evil one, we know that to be Satan, as mentioned earlier, is the god of this world. And if the world is under his control, then evil is going to happen. We shouldn't be bewildered by the absurdity of this world, but we should know who is at the core of it. However, the God of Abraham, Isaac, and Jacob, the same God who freed the Israelites from Egypt and who is the God of Israel to this day, has not left us helpless. He gave us the fruit-producing Word that has provided us with a fountain of resources, from reading it to crafting scriptures to music to strengthen our character in Him. God is the one who makes us new and sets us apart from this world.

As we cleanse our minds, we continue to become new creatures set apart from the world; old, secular thoughts, habits, and attitudes should be shed from us as a rebirth happens in our heart, and we become new people in Christ per 2 Corinthians 5:17. Notice I said should have been shed because for some they have not let go of old, secular thoughts, habits, and attitudes that continue to weigh them down in their minds and influence their faith. That is the great shift that should have happened in all our lives if we profess to be Christ followers—the shift from old, devious, worldly habits, thoughts, and attitudes to something beautifully refined and made new. It's a spiritual cleansing that can happen as we immerse ourselves in God's Word. Let's reflect on two spiritual men in the Bible, one from the Old Testament and the other from the New, who were mighty men, conservators for the people, blameless before God and yet at times surrounded by opposition on all sides. They were persecuted, and people murmured against them, but they never forsook their faith in God. And subsequently, they were given power by God to do His will. They were both considered deliverers. They consecrated themselves to God and spent time hearing from Him for direction as a way to cleanse their mind from all the rhetoric around them. They are examples we should follow in renewing our mind in the Word.

Chapter 13

A Refreshing through Renewing and Communing

These two holy men referenced in the previous chapter are Moses and Jesus, both similar in having unimpeachable reputations for being coworkers for God. These two historic symbols have been able to remain inculpable amid persecution because of their time laboring before God. Moses does eventually succumb to pressure and sin when he smote a rock twice instead of speaking to it out of his frustration toward the people complaining (Numbers 20:8–12); however, prior to that event, he remains righteous before God. God sent Moses to Egypt to deliver the Israelite slaves from Egyptian rule, and that is the same God who sent Jesus to the world to deliver us from satanic rule. Moses has his first encounter with God after he flees from Egypt and meets a Midianite woman who becomes his wife before being called to return to Egypt as a deliverer. Moses, a Hebrew by birth, grows up as an Egyptian prince, then becomes a slave momentarily, finds himself communing with God for the first time as he is called toward a burning bush on the backside of the desert by an angel of God. As an Egyptian prince, he was exposed to pagan gods as the indigenous people of Egypt did during that time. How is it that this former prince, for a moment a slave, then a nomad, finds himself in an appointment with the God of the universe? It's only by God's divine authority. So Moses ascends upon the bush, and the Lord calls him by name, to which he replies, "Here am I" (Exodus 3:1–4, KJV). I pause here for a second just to focus on the words "Here am I" and try to think of the last time you have said that to the Lord. As God attempts to get our attention sometimes just to commune with Him and bring restoration to our mind,

He just might call our names, but we have to be sensitive enough to hear and respond to Him. Moses, who didn't even know God, is having this profound yet awe-inspiring rendezvous with Him. We need moments like this with our Lord. This is a pivotal moment in Moses' life when God calls his name twice, but he also responds with "Here am I." He is recognizing God's voice, although this is his first time speaking with the Lord in this type of encounter, and yet he yields to the authority and sovereignty of his Maker by responding and then following the next instructions given by God. He was to draw closer and take off his shoes because the place where he was standing was holy ground (verse 5). During that time with God on the backside of the desert mountain, Moses is educated about the affliction of the Hebrew slaves. He is called to be a deliverer, learns that God is the "I AM," and though he comes up with multiple reasons why he is not the right person, God encourages him, provides a supporter through his brother Aaron, then gives him the power to carry out these plans. As the story of Moses unfolds, he does go unto Pharaoh, who refuses to free the slaves, and has another encounter with God, who promises to deliver Israel as Moses finds himself losing hope (Exodus 5: 22–23, 6:1–8). He has to constantly go back to seek God's face, hear from Him, and follow His instructions. He returns to Pharaoh and is met with the same resistance but is given instructions by God to perform a miracle, to which Pharaoh calls his magicians to do the same (Exodus 7:9–11). Moses communes with God for more insight and instructions, and that's when he turns the water into blood (Exodus 7:14–17). Various plagues affected Egypt prior to Pharaoh eventually letting the Hebrew slaves go free; however, note that each time an affliction happened, it was proceeded by Moses communing with God. He never pronounced any plague or performed any miracle, even in the desert, without renewing his mind and spending time with God first. This is how he knew what to do, not in his own power but by hearing from God and cleansing his mind. In the wilderness, Moses is enjoying time with God even when the Israelites are complaining and being rebellious. The most noteworthy is when the Lord initiated the first sequence of renewing the mind practice with Moses in the first battle with Amalek. Joshua defeats Amalek as Moses' hands are held up with support from Aaron and Hur (Exodus 17:8–13). In verse 14 is where we see the Lord at work as He instructs Moses in renewing the mind, "And the Lord said unto Moses, Write this for a memorial in a book, and rehearse it in the ears of Joshua: for I will utterly put out the remembrance of Amalek from under heaven." The act of writing in a book and rehearsing in the ears is an act of renewing the mind, cleansing the combative thoughts, and re-centering those thoughts toward God. Writing it down is remembrance, and rehearsing is renewing. These are not the only steps God took toward showing Moses how to cleanse his mind. During the moments at Mount Sinai, where Israel rose up in insurrection against God, but Moses sought peace and refuge with Him, he understood that reverential time with the Lord is an act of renewing the mind. He wasn't seeking protection from the Israelites. He was in need of preservation for his spirit. He spends multiple hours communing with God on Mount Sinai. During that first encounter at Mount Sinai, the Lord shares with Moses a covenant that he is to lay out before the people of Israel. Israel accepts the New Covenant, and Moses conveys that to the Lord, who tells him to have the people sanctify themselves (Exodus 19:10–11). Moses receives the Ten Commandments. According to the Bible, there are about 613 entire commandments (Exodus 20:3–17), and in Exodus 24:3, Israel consents to do all that the Lord has laid out in the commandments. In Exodus 24:18, the communion begins with God for forty days and nights as the tablets of stone are drafted for the Ten Commandments.

During that forty-year period, wandering around the wilderness (Joshua 5:6), Moses continued to commune with God. He was contrite in heart and mind, even knowing he would not step foot into the Promised Land as he was giving Joshua instructions on what to do next. Only God could enable him to handle what would never be for him with humility and grace. He's not crying, "Lord, please, consider me," or begging Him to go into the Promised Land. He accepts it. We also need to be humble enough to accept the plans God has for us, and that only comes through renewing the mind in God's Word so His thoughts are adopted as our thoughts. Then, we will follow Him. Jesus experiences a similar encounter with His Father in the wilderness before being called into ministry. Matthew 4:1–11 is the teaching of how to manage temptation from the enemy, as Jesus was also tempted after spending time communing and consecrating Himself to God for forty days and nights.

There is a parallel in terms of time frame with both Moses and Jesus. The significance of forty comes up again as both spend that amount of time having fellowship with God. Could it be that this is the example time frame for us as well? That period of time is what it might take for us to renew our minds in God's presence, and for some, it could be longer. This sets the stage right before Jesus takes on the ministry and life-altering task that God gave His Son to do. He has a confrontation with the devil, who makes three propositions to Jesus, and He doesn't fall for any of the temptations, but the greatest part about that passage is the ministering angels that come to Him to provide comfort and care for Jesus' needs. The angels come in place of the devil, as indicated in some translations, as they replace the demonic presence with the positive and good presence only given by God. The presence of angels is significant here. It goes back to the previous discussion and predisposition about there being joy in the presence of angels. I can only imagine that after this impious encounter, Jesus was in need of some joy as the ministering angels cared for His needs, likely both spiritually and physically, by ensuring His needs are met. I am so thankful to God for the ministering angels, even the ones with us today, as they provide joy after persecuting and vexing situations occur. I definitely believe ministering angels are present today. This ushers in Jesus' teaching career, which only lasted three years of His adult life. I like to think of it as one year for the Father, one year for the Son, Himself, and one year for the Holy Spirit. The famous sermon on the mount and the teaching of the Beatitudes, defined in King James as a state of blessedness, is the inauguration of His servitude on behalf of God, His Father. We will not review all of the Beatitudes, but there is one scripture in chapter 5 that speaks to cleansing and renewing the mind, and that is verse 8 (KJV), "Blessed are the pure in heart: for they shall see God." As I was taught many years ago by my pastor, Christine Miles, the only way to have a pure heart is through renewing the mind. By cross-referencing this scripture in the Message translation, it states, "You're blessed when you get your inside world—your mind and heart—put right. Then you can see God in the outside world." This speaks specifically about the mind but also adds the heart as part of this getting right process. We can only "put ourselves right" by renewing the mind. It is the purification process that Jesus is relating to in this scripture. The terms and conditions for how we renew our mind are talked about in chapter 6 regarding prayer and fasting. Jesus teaches us how to pray through the model prayer (Matthew 6:5–15) and about fasting (vv. 16–18). We are to pray without ceasing (1 Thessalonians 5:16–18) and fast until we see change to bring our body under submission and discipline (1 Corinthians 9:27). How often are you praying and fasting to grow closer to God and purifying your thoughts, heart, and attitude toward your heavenly Father? I think this is so important because, at times, we blame God for circumstances that are not His fault, or the enemy is ardently hammering our thoughts so that we want to scapegoat God for what really belongs to the enemy. It is by his doing that wicked and horrible things happen. Prayer and fasting remind us of the goodness of God and His vast love for us. It is so important that we don't get bogged down by the weight of the world or earthly circumstances. Jesus didn't, and He is our sample Son to follow. He spent a vast majority of His time in prayer to the Father so that He could consult Him before doing anything as He discloses to the disciples in John 5:19 that He can do nothing by Himself but only what the Father tells Him to do, and in John 12:49, He doesn't say anything apart from what His Father tells Him to say. This is evidence that points to Jesus spending time with the Father. He must have spent time with God to know what His Father wanted Him to say and do. The washing and cleansing process for Jesus occurs when He spends time with God so He never becomes completely weighed down by idle and worldly temptations and persecutions. Instead, He was able to remain in the presence of God, only doing and saying as His Father did. We can also see hints of this idea of renewing the mind in Matthew 6:24–34 about putting God's kingdom first. The more we put God's kingdom first in everything we do, the more we can see His goodness in all that we do and not the deception of the enemy trying to tell us otherwise. Seek God first, His kingdom, and His righteousness, and everything will be added to you. Seek Him first in thought, attitude, and behavior. We sometimes ask ourselves, "What is the attitude of God?" which is the same as saying, "What is the heart of God?" It's seeking His principles first and walking in love. Jesus came to teach the principles of God's Word and bring the hearts or the attitudes of the ungodly back to the Father. He came as the model for us, the sample Son and one true Adam, unlike the first who fell to temptation. Jesus wants us to follow after Him. Jesus sacrificed His life to atone for our sins, thereby washing and sanctifying us back to the Father. And since we have been ransomed back through the crucifixion of Christ, then we can seek the Father's face first in everything without guilt or shame. Romans 8:1 reminds us of this very promise.

Taking some steps back from Jesus' crucifixion and resurrection, let's look at Jesus' miracle ministry as He seeks the Father's face before doing anything. Jesus is descending from the mountain after ministering the Beatitudes and is followed by a leper who is beseeching Jesus for healing. The Chrism of God was moving during Jesus' teaching, so God was already present with Him when this leper approached. The man asks, "If though wilt, thou canst make me clean" (Matthew 8:2b, KJV). He is asking the desire and will of God, which Jesus interprets and fulfills the heart of the Father by responding "I will" in verse 3. This might be a stretch for some, but my thought is that the only way Jesus knew the will of God is by intimately knowing and spending time with Him. He doesn't respond with "I will think about it." He immediately knew the Father's desire and predisposition for healing. He had consulted with God already during the anointed sermon on the mount. When the anointing of God is flowing, He is present in the atmosphere, and thus, Jesus had already been in God's presence to know His desire. Jesus heals several more, including a centurion's servant and Peter's mother-in-law, before calming a storm and assessing the fear of His disciples who haven't yet adopted the heart and mind of Christ (Matthew 8:23–27, KJV). Jesus is fast asleep on this turbulent sea, and the disciples come to wake Him. He views the situation and immediately says, "Why are ye fearful, O ye of little faith?" This is where we first learn from the sample Son that fear and faith cannot operate in the same vessel, and He also has an appraisal of their fear as a lack of faith, which we can equate to not trusting Jesus. Essentially, the disciples were saying we didn't trust the anointing power of Jesus when they were waking Him up in a state of anxiety. We will talk more about fear and trust in the next section, as it does affect our level of joy. However, note that Jesus rebukes the wind and the sea to calm the storm. Now, the focus here is not on Jesus calming the storm or even the fear factor but more on the fact that Jesus was asleep. This speaks yet again to the terms and conditions of renewing the mind and the importance of slumber as a way to reset our mind, attitude, and thoughts back to the Father. Many books and studies can reveal the value of sleep. Some notable ones are *Why We Sleep* by Matthew Walker, PhD, and *The Nocturnal Brain* by Dr. Guy Leschiziner. The quality and quantity of our sleep are also significant as proper rest helps us to relax our mind, provides us the ability to imagine, obtain vision, receive direction, and surrender this altered state of consciousness to God if we are Christ followers. Jesus sleeping in this scripture is of great substance to us but often overlooked as one of the conditions for renewing the mind. In His slumber, He was renewing and communing with God, so when He wakes to see the storm, He can stay in a state of peace, unlike the disciples who were fearful. He heard from God on what to do in this storm. Don't think for a moment that sleep is not important and sometimes the only way God can minister and commune with some of us as we pretend to be too busy to spend any time renewing our mind when awake. In that time of slumber, Jesus is hearing God's thoughts and predilections; thus, He is woken in a panic by His disciples, but He remains calm, including being faithful to His Father, and speaks peace during this storm. While resting, God helps us to transpose our thoughts for His thoughts so we are ready for whatever comes. Essentially, He is giving us what to think when we refresh our thoughts in the Word.

Jesus spends time in prayer before calling His twelve apostles. When I was a child, I always heard this story about Jesus calling the twelve but never understood how He knew who to call. My thought is that being a disciple is a great responsibility, but being an ordained apostle of Christ carries a great mantle of stewardship authority. It's not just assigned to anyone, but Jesus was strategic about His choice. I see this first in Matthew 10:1–4, where it was often taught, but as I parallel that scripture with Luke 6:12–13 (NLT), I learned that Jesus had gone into a mountain to pray and did so all night. At daybreak is when He makes His selection of the twelve apostles from the multitude of disciples. He knew who to call because He had spent time in prayer, an act of renewing His mind. So, again, we are given a prototype of the prerequisites of renewing the mind. When we adopt God's thoughts and heart, He provides direction on what to do during times of influential selections and ponderous choices. Jesus knew exactly what to do and likely didn't hesitate in making His selection because He had prayed all night until daybreak before calling the apostles. Jesus only considered what God told Him to consider and do, nothing more and nothing less. In Matthew 14:22–33 (AMP), Jesus goes to the disciples walking on water.

> *"Immediately He directed the disciples to get into the boat and go ahead of Him to the other side [of the Sea of Galilee], while He sent the crowds away. After He had dismissed the crowds, He went up on the mountain by Himself to pray. When it was evening, He was there alone. But the boat [by this time] was already a long distance from land, tossed and battered by the waves; for the wind was against them. And in the fourth watch of the night (3:00–6:00 a.m.) Jesus came to them, walking on the sea. When the disciples saw Him walking on the sea, they were terrified, and said, "It is a ghost!" And they cried out in fear. But immediately He spoke to them, saying, "Take courage, it is I! Do not be afraid!" Peter replied to Him, "Lord, if it is [really] You, command me to come to You on the water." He said, "Come!" So Peter got out of the boat, and walked on the water and came toward Jesus. But when he saw [the effects of] the wind, he was frightened, and he began to sink, and he cried out, "Lord, save me!" Immediately Jesus extended His hand and caught him, saying to him, "O you of little faith, why did you doubt?" And when they got into the boat, the wind ceased. Then those in the boat worshiped Him [with awe-inspired reverence], saying, "Truly You are the Son of God!""*

There is one important word in this passage that gets overlooked, and that's the word "immediately." Each time something contrary to the faith that Jesus wanted His disciples to possess happened, He immediately responded. When they see Him walking on the water, they become afraid, and Jesus, sensing that in His spirit, immediately speaks to them, and what He says is to edify and encourage their faith. He doesn't allow the fear to fester for a while before saying, "Take courage, it is I." Instead, the scripture says, "But immediately He spoke to them." A condition of us renewing our mind is that when a contrary thought tries to take residence in your mind, you have to "but immediately" speak to it. Jesus does the same with Peter when He begins to walk toward Him on the water, but Peter, "seeing the effects of the wind, becomes frightened and begins to sink." Peter cries out, "Lord, save me!" And immediately, Jesus responds by extending His hand. Notice how Jesus ensures physical safety first, calms the person, and then course corrects. He says to Peter, "O you of little faith, why did you doubt?" The extended caption underneath this says, "Why did you allow yourself to be drawn in two directions?" So Peter was being drawn in two directions: one of believing and one of doubting. When our thoughts and behavior do not align with our beliefs or, in this instance, our faith, we can be drawn in two different directions, also leading to what I refer to as *spiritual cognitive dissonance*. When we see our thoughts and behaviors not matching our faith, we need to react immediately, just as Jesus did, to renew our mind back to our faith in God's Word. The longer we wait to respond, the wavering in our thoughts and behavior against our faith will not only create cognitive dissonance, but it also becomes less pliable for God to renew our mind back to Him. The Bible also reminds us not to give the enemy place, which we can do even in our thoughts. Stop entertaining the doubt, the disbelief, the junk. Look for the immediacy of God's response and then His correction in any situation. Be sensitive to hearing from Him, and the best way to do that is to cleanse your mind in the Word and then respond immediately to that perverse thought. Lastly, let's look at the feast of Passover meal Jesus is having with His disciples found in Matthew 26:26–30, where He instructs the disciples to partake symbolically of Him through the eating of the bread to reflect His body and the drinking of the wine to represent His blood. This is what we are to do in remembrance of Him and as an act of our covenant with Jesus. Most of us engage in this sacrosanct practice regularly on Sundays at church, but we may not be aware of the exponential power it holds in fortifying our minds back to the sacrifice Jesus made for us. As we remain in covenant with God through our Lord Jesus by taking the sacraments, we honor and remember the covenant He created with us so that we are not living as the world lives but recalling what Jesus did for us to have eternal life. Through Jesus' death, we are set free in our minds yet become enslaved again by living in this world, thinking as they think, and practicing things contrary to our faith. Why is that? I think living in this world demands us to be challenged by our thoughts and behavior to ensure they align with our faith at every crossing. We can learn through the practice of our faith that any thought that does not bring the flow of joy, we have the authority to cast it down. Moses' ministry in the wilderness taught us the importance of renewing the mind for miraculous transactions to occur between us and God. Moses and Jesus' ministry taught us how to renew the mind through specific terms and conditions such as fasting initially, then prayer, teaching and preaching, rest, communing with God through the sacraments, and the immediacy of us to act when we recognize controversy in our beliefs and thoughts. You have to act to change the current of joy you want to receive; possibly something more you have to do or something less you should not be doing. Ask the Holy Spirit for guidance when trying to discern what to do, and He will assist you. You asking the Holy Spirit is not only giving Him an assignment, it's also you taking an action step.

Chapter 14

A Refreshing of Your Thoughts through the Word

Let's review the steps God took to bring us back in right standing with him as a way for our joy to be fulfilled. So, the first step God took to demonstrate His love was sending His Son, Jesus. Secondly, Jesus descends to hell to defeat Satan and disarm his minions so he has no dominion over us, not even in our thoughts (Colossians 2:15). But for extra measure and as a gift, God gave us the Holy Spirit, so we would not be alone. He also gifted us with heavenly tongues so we can speak directly to Him without interruption or interpretation by the enemy. This is an uncontaminated yet reverential way for us to commune with God, and the Bible refers to it as a spiritual gift. Lastly, God gave us the Bible, His Word and our sword. Take the word and add an "s" to it, and it becomes a sword when we need a weapon or the Word when we need encouragement. This world contains both good and evil, and sometimes we will not go unscathed from these evil affairs; however, those who are Christ followers can meditate on Romans 8:28 and know God is working all things together for their good. Christ came to save us from the god of this world, and our sovereign and transcendent God gave us His Word so that with all the pernicious happenings in this world, we can refresh and renew our minds in the Word to shed the pain, hurt, anger, and whatever else holds us back from experiencing that joy that God promised us. Joy is found in His scriptures, unspeakable and unadulterated joy. In the beginning was the Word, and the Word was with God, and the Word was God. And guess what? The Word still stands to this day (John 1:1). God and the Word are one. Metaphorically, God's Word is our body wash, our soap, and whatever else we use to cleanse ourselves. It cleanses our thoughts (the mind), our hearts (the spirit), and our attitudes. But before God could cleanse us, He had to bring us back in line with Him, and when we accept Christ, that is an act of us cleansing ourselves. Then, we continue to cleanse ourselves through the Word. It is a daily washing that removes the debris that can get stuck on us from living in this iniquitous world and allows us not to forget His Word nor to omit walking according to His Word.

Remember, faith comes by hearing and hearing by the Word of God (Romans 10:17), and the just [the Christ follower] is expected to live by faith (Hebrews 10:38), so as I see it, the Word is God, and God and faith are one, and faith is the Word. Thus, as believers, we are to be the Word. We can't be the Word if we don't know it or wash ourselves in the Word daily. As believers, we get dirty in this world because the persecution is great, but the Bible reminds us not to draw back because His soul will not take pleasure in that person. We are not to be like those who draw back unto perdition, but we are to be like those believing in the saving of the soul (Hebrews 10:38–39). Don't draw back because the persecution is great. Just continue holding onto the faith and washing yourself in the Word. It's not easy to do when we feel like we are carrying the weight of the world, but that is specifically why the Bible warns us of what is to come and gives a way out through renewing our mind, casting our cares, and being a warrior like David through prayer and praise. We are the Word in our actions and thoughts, and we continue to be cleansed by it in whatever way we choose to honor God. It is a maturation process that takes place in our thoughts, attitudes, and hearts. The Bible tells us to set our mind and keep it set habitually on things that are above, not on this earth (Colossians 3:2). In this way, when the debris gets thrown around, we stay focused on heavenly things, not on temporal things on this earth. I am not saying that we are not to have an emotional response to these earthly Christian molestations and traumatic atrocities; however, we are not to react to it the same way as the world does. We are to firmly and wholeheartedly maintain our joy and smile. We cannot let our hearts be troubled or afraid, as the Bible reminds us, but we must believe in the Father. Our response has to be to maintain that higher level thinking, being filled with grace in our hearts, and having a spirit or attitude of Christ that only comes from spending time with him. We might be rejected, afflicted, and maltreated, but we need to know the spirit God has called us to function in, and as we cleanse ourselves, it helps us exemplify that spirit even when these happenings occur. In Luke 9:51–56, Jesus is headed with His disciples to a Samaritan village. His destination is Jerusalem. And He sends messengers before Him to prepare for His coming, but He was not well received. The disciples John and James have a nullifying afterthought. Verses 54–56 (AMP),

> *"They said, 'Lord, do you want us to command fire to come down from heaven and destroy them?' But he turned and rebuked them [and He said, 'You do not know what kind of spirit you are, for the Son of Man did not come to destroy men's lives, but to save them"] And they journeyed on to another village."*

We have to maintain the right spirit, a spirit like Jesus. Do you know what spirit you are of? If for a second you hesitated to answer that question for yourself, you likely need to refresh your mind in the Word. This can be the metric that we all use to determine whether a thorough cleansing in God's Word is necessary. If you notice your spirit is not mimicking God's spirit or you are calling fire down from heaven, it might be time for a washing of your mind in the Word of God. Your spirit should be imitative of God's spirit, despite being received by others or not. Your goal is not to be received by people on this earth anyway but to rejoice when we are received in heaven. We have to journey on to the next place when we are not received, just as Jesus did with His disciples. This is yet another example of how Jesus handled conflict and rejection. It's something we can apply to our lives in a pragmatic way.

Another reason to refresh ourselves in the Word is substantiated through scripture, "But be ye doers of the word, and not hearers only, deceiving your own selves" (James 1:22, KJV). As noted previously, we cannot do the Word unless we know the Word, just like we cannot teach what we don't know. We spend a lot of time getting obese physically, but we need to be obese spiritually. We need to feed on the Word to fill our spirits. There are so many avenues and spiritual leaders for us to have a buffet on the Word. The way to share the cleansing of the Word with others is for us to do the Word we know to do ourselves. We know it because we study it and feed our spirits on it daily. Listening to the Word is great. But the Word we do is greater. Perhaps another way to measure whether a renewing of the mind is needed is by introspection, whether you are a doer of the Word or a hearer only. Are you putting the Word into action? When is the last time you have fed your spirit? As we begin to do the Word we hear and learn, we can share the joy of our salvation with others. We can help them walk with fervid strength in this world. We can put them on assignment for Christ instead of the enemy of this world. The question is, how do we do the Word? That is a question with many parts because doing the Word does not contain one philosophical thought, activity, or proposition. It is a myriad of specific theological, psychological, and spiritual approaches to prepare us for the advent of Christ. Doing the Word is essentially living the Word, walking in the way of the Word, talking the Word, and having a mindset of the Word. An example of walking in the way of the Word can be found in Genesis 3. God told Adam not to eat of the fruit from a tree in the midst of the Garden of Eden. Adam was given a directive by the Almighty, and yet when his wife saw the fruit as "good for food" and "pleasant to the eyes," she gave it to him to eat, and he did partake. At that very moment, they committed patricide, not as we think of it in the natural as killing one's father, but spiritual patricide as in spoiling or marring God with their bad performance and representation of Him. They rejected Him as their spiritual Father, being preoccupied and enticed by the enemy. One way for us to do the Word, even from the book of Genesis, is to recognize that everything that looks good for food and pleasant to the eyes or appetizing is not good for us. Some folks may look at this as just food, the fruit not to eat, but I believe this instruction is applied generally throughout our life. It's not just appealing food. It could be sex appeal, professional appeal, neighborhood appeal, financial appeal, etcetera. If we are going to do the Word, we must be able to hear from God about what not to eat. Everything pleasant to the eyes is not good for you. This creation story is one example of how to do the Word. The very first example can be found in Genesis 1:3 when God said, "Let there be light." He spoke the Word and spoke light into the darkness, an example to us of how to speak the Word. As we do the Word and refresh our hearts, attitudes, and thoughts in the Word, we can speak light into our darkness as well. We can resist the temptation of committing patricide against our heavenly Father. It's strategic for us to understand how to do the Word and comprehend Scripture in the totality of its meaning. The Word is alive and active, as scripture tells us. We give it more life as we walk in it by following the Word and live it by doing the Word in deed and thinking elevated thoughts. This might include casting down certain thoughts and bringing other thoughts captive to be obedient with Christ's thoughts. The Word is our strategy against the enemy.

When I was a program director at The Bridge Family Center, I recall asking all the staff to admonish the children to shower as a cathartic process, wash in the morning to start the day, and in the evening to wash off the cares of the day. Some of the youth appreciated that concept and would quickly shower off a bad day, but others needed convincing. However, we noticed the more we promoted it, the more we gained buy-in from them to do it, and they believed it to be working. Some would ask to take a shower before we would begin the transition meeting with the youth, from morning staff change over to afternoon staff. Staff noticed that the youth seemed more attuned and receptive after showering before our meetings, as did I. Showering is cathartic, particularly a hot shower, and especially when it's cold. Showering is a way to symbolically wash away the debris slung at us throughout the day or possibly a reset to relax for the evening. I think it's so important to bookend our day by spiritually washing our minds, thoughts, and hearts in the Word of God each day. Our mind doesn't stay renewed daily any more than our stomach stays full daily. We are asked multiple times throughout scripture to meditate on God's Word and renew our mind. Why? Because our thoughts are shaped every day by what we hear and the experiences we have. In order to get back to a place of joy, we have to renew our mind in God's Word, a washing away, a cleansing of all the "stuff" we experience daily. Then, meditate on that Word and immerse ourselves in the Word until we see change in the natural. The Bible tells us to think on these things that are lovely, pure, and so on per Philippians 4:9. This is part of the Thinking Test, as previously mentioned. Renewing my mind is an act of self-care so that I can think on the things of the Bible instead of being focused on worldly things. I renew my mind for me because, without it, I couldn't function in this world or maintain being a coworker for Christ. It is because I care for myself that I renew my mind in the word as a demonstration of my faith in God. I know that His Word will see me through whatever is going on better than having drinks with friends, drowning my sorrows in a movie, eating my favorite meal, and certainly last longer than a back massage, a hot shower, or doing yoga. His Word is magnanimous, electrifying, miraculous, activating and has lasted through the ages and will continue to be a steady foundation for us to fortify our thoughts to become mentally healthy. It is an invitation to God to take up root in our minds, germinate in our hearts, consequently producing fruit in our behavior. Spending that time with God immersed in His Word is life-changing. You wonder why your joy remains when all hell is breaking loose around you because you have renewed your mind in God's Word. A renewed mind stays in a place of joy. Seek Him first. That is what His Word asks of us. The more we choose to put God first and renew our mind, the more we are choosing to care for ourselves rather than allowing our hearts to be hardened by the cares of this world. We actually are saving ourselves from worry, fear, and whatever else the enemy is waiting to launch at us.

Some might be thinking, "Well, what about the persecution that the Bible talks about and even the disciples of Christ hold as truth for us? I say to that, "The Bible, God's written Word, didn't promise us persecution. It is prompting us about it. The enemy wants to take us out and not to dinner. His goal is to destroy us because we believe the truth and because of our faith, trust, and love for God. This prompting comes based on the fall of man and the initial sin, thus the warning of persecution because of the evil that exists in the hearts of many. This is to forearm us for what to expect." Isaiah 59:15 (NLT), "Yes, truth is gone, and anyone who renounces evil is attacked. The Lord looked and was displeased to find there was no justice." If you live the truth, attacks might come, but God has given us the Word to intervene for us, and in Romans 8, Jesus and the Holy Spirit are doing intercession for us. So Paul advises about persecution, but don't hold onto that only. God's promises for us are sweet, generous, and merciful. We are warned of persecutions to come so we are not stupefied by them; however, God promised us joy found in several scriptures in His Word. Joy is a promise of God, and everything He promised, we can have. Take God's written Word and make it a real word by speaking it over yourself. That is the active Word of God. I will have joy. It is mine. And when I smile, I release that joy to others.

Chapter 15

Move Over...Make Room

We have to make room for joy to come into our lives. It's not simply by desiring it, but we have to abandon and eliminate some things that have caused emotional and psychological wounds, vexatious afflictions, or spiritual strongholds so that we can feel joy. Every experience we have, whether good or bad, leaves an imprint on us. The bad likely creates disdain, and the residue left behind from it can be shame or hurt, feelings of inferiority or insecurity, sorrow or resentment, but we have to let it go to make room for the merriment in life. It's our promise as Christ followers despite what has happened to us or what the enemy tries to dissuade us of. Remind yourself that joy is yours and receive it as one of the gifts God has promised you by faith. Although it is promised to us just as there are many promises in the Bible, we may miss it for many reasons, but not everyone receives all the promises acclaimed in the Bible. For example, God's Word promises us grace through faith, but if we never receive faith in the gospel and the finished works of the cross, then we will never receive grace for ourselves for the things we have done or extend grace to others. Sometimes, that is the problem. We don't comprehend this grace promise or only partly receive the grace gift instead of fully inheriting it. We are also promised healing under this grace gift, but not everyone receives healing. Provision is another promise, but we all don't receive that either (Matthew 6:33). But the Bible tells us in 2 Corinthians 1:20 that all of God's promises are "yes" and "Amen." I repeated this scripture for its strength in holding onto God's promises when the enemy tries to talk you out of what our salvation has promised us through the grace gift. God did not promise us an explanation or disclosure of His plans for us, nor does He have to. He is God. But He did promise us He would be with us, never leave us, and He also promised us guidance. If you are going through a tough time, just know that God is with you, He has not forsaken you, and as you continue to profess your joy in God's Word, you are moving hellish enterprises and demonic powers out of the way to make room for joyous endeavors.

Joy is ours. It was secured for us, but we have to make room for it and be prepared to receive it in all of its fullness: in comprehension, in rest, in declaration, in activity, in obedience, and in faith. This metaphor seems to be the most applicable here. It's the idea of someone making room in their closet to buy new clothes. If your closet is congested, you have to purge to make room for the new clothes. Why is it that purging a closet seems so logical to do, but we forget to do that when it comes to things like joy? Is it because clothes are more tangible? But joy is just as tangible in laughter and smiling. It is because we put clothes on? I had to refute that also because we can put on a smile. Moreover, it's not just in a smile that we put on joy. We have to put it on in our mind as a determinant desire by exposing ourselves to joyful things, we put it on in our thoughts by having cheerful thinking habits, in how we feel it is palpable, and we put it on in our actions by smiling or even with our eyes or other facial expressions beyond smiling, that's how it shows up for others. Cleaning out one's closet to make room for new clothes is a well-known and adapted concept, and not well-known for something like joy. I recall when working on my own joy journey that the Holy Spirit said to me it would never work the way I was doing it. I didn't fully understand at first. Why wouldn't it work? The answer to that question didn't come until seeking the Holy Spirit further in prayer. The Holy Spirit explained that no one can have a negative thought life and a negative attitude yet experience heavenly joy. He gave me the analogy of cleaning out the closet to make room for new clothes. I was thinking, cleaning my closet out to purge clothes is an easy task, but clearing out my thoughts and attitude to only be positive might be tougher. Well, that's what I thought, looking at it from the natural instead of the spirit. But I learned years ago to rebuke the negative I hear and to cast down thoughts that don't align with God's thoughts. The Holy Spirit said, "There is nothing new I am asking of you. It's literally what you have been doing, but do it with more fervor and consistency." When I first notice my thoughts or attitude becoming negative, I immediately need to do something about it. The action included casting down those negative thoughts that were contributing to a negative attitude. I cast it down by speaking to it, recognizing the negative thought exists, then challenging it against God's Word. Every foreign thought was rebuked. And if you find yourself unsure whether a thought is negative, you have a few options: either go to the Bible to search if that thought is accurate per the Word or ask the Holy Spirit, who will not steer you wrong. As I started purging my thought life, I was able to make room for positive thoughts to infiltrate my mind, contributing to a more positive attitude. But the most important part of this operation was to never let a thought remain stagnant. When I began to do that, I noticed the joy of God penetrating my thoughts even more. We have to clean the closet of our mind from the negative to make room for what's new. It's the same concept with most things in life. We have to release something to make room for something else. Our thoughts work that way as well. Holding onto polarizing thoughts is challenging. Eventually, one thought has to be abated to make room for the new thought. If you have discouraging thoughts, you have to make room for joyful thoughts if you want to change your frame of mind. Make room in your thought process for joy, make room in your spirit for joy, make room in your emotions for joy, and make room in your life for joy. How do you make room in your thoughts for joy? It's by renewing your mind, as we discussed previously. Rid your mind of those negative thoughts to make room for new ones. We cannot be of two minds, as the scripture persuades us in James 1:8. Do not be given over to a depraved mind (Romans 1:28) by not acknowledging God. It's worthwhile for us to acknowledge Him in our thoughts and actions. Philippians 4:7–9 (NIV) states,

> *"And the peace of God, which transcends all understanding, will guard your hearts and your minds in Christ Jesus. Finally, brothers and sisters, whatever is true, whatever is noble, whatever is right, whatever is pure, whatever is lovely, whatever is admirable—if anything is excellent or praiseworthy—think about such things.*

Whatever you have learned or received or heard from me, or seen in me—put it into practice. And the God of peace will be with you."

This is a godly memo to us of what to think on whenever we have lost our way or forgotten the character of God's thoughts. Additionally, we are reminded to practice what has been learned, received, and heard, and as we practice, God's peace is with us. So, if you find yourself without peace, look back on this scripture. What do you need to do, and how can you make it practically apply to your life? Practicing this scripture is a skillful and prudent way to clean up your thoughts and make room for new, joyful thoughts.

Let's focus on how we will make room in our spirit, emotions, and life for this heavenly joy. Remember, we are spirit beings. We possess a soul and live in a physical body. We are immortal spirits just like our Creator, God Elohim, and our spirit connects with Him just as His spirit connects with us. So, if we need to make room in our spirit for joy, then we need to link up with God's spirit by using our faith. We can link our spirit to God's spirit by staying connected to the vine, who is Jesus, the Son of God, staying in God's presence, and staying in a place of Eden, most of which we have talked about. But pragmatically, how can we link to God's spirit when we are doing everything we know to do, such as reading the Bible, praying, and fasting, but not feeling His presence or a change in our spirit...? The answer is to be patient and consistent. I would also recommend walking in love as part of the New Testament commandment. It's one of the fastest ways to connect your spirit to God because when your love is demonstrated, especially during persecuting moments, your faith is employed, and faith comes from Him. Ardent praise and worship, which draws us nearer to God as we sing from the heart in gratitude and honor to Him, is another form of connecting your spirit to God hastily. We also need to know that God's presence is with us even if we don't feel Him or audibly hear from Him. He is with you anyway. He will not leave you (Deuteronomy 31:6–8, Joshua 1:5, Psalm 55:22, Isaiah 41:10, Matthew 28:20, Hebrews 13:5–6, Revelations 3:10–12). His Word never tells us our five senses need to be regaled in an effort for His presence to be with us. The just shall live by faith (Romans 1:17), not our five senses. He is with us always, even until the end of this age. And His silence doesn't mean He's not working. Actually, God is always speaking to us through the Holy Spirit, but we may not always be hearing Him in our spirit. Some may be looking for a sign or an audible voice when they really need to connect their spirit to God. The heart is what connects us to God, not our five senses. Stir up your own spirit in the Word. Many times, folks are not consistent enough or not patient enough, and sometimes, not seeing God in something that He actually had a hand in, though we are looking in the wrong direction. Remember, the direction of joy comes from looking at God. Faithfulness is demonstrated by our consistency and patience. However, if we want to fast-track our way into God's presence, the best way I would suggest is by praying in the spirit. It is our direct line of communication with Him. We have all been given that ability and authority to pray in tongues when we became born again and accepted Jesus as Lord of our lives as the Holy Spirit entered in, but this is also another example of a weapon we have been promised but often don't use enough. Praying in our heavenly language is an unparalleled way of receiving and hearing from the Lord. It's transcendent and herculean. It's actually refreshing when feeling exhausted and joyous when feeling sad. I have experienced this for myself, either feeling tired and as soon as I begin praying in the spirit, I receive nourishment for my soul or feeling bereaved then suddenly feeling a burst of hope. Nothing surpasses being in the presence of God, and by praying in the Spirit, we can quickly get into His presence and connect our spirit with His spirit. It's impossible to pray in the Spirit and not have your spirit linked to His because we need the Spirit of God (the Holy Spirit) to use our heavenly prayer language. We need to hear encouraging words in our spirit to build us up, and I found that the most remarkable way to do it is by speaking in tongues when I perceive myself to be out of options. If I can't sit and read the Word, declare it while pacing the floor, or get into His presence with praise and worship, I will pray in tongues. It works every time. Ever found yourself so upset you couldn't connect to God's spirit evening reading the Bible? That's when occupying by speaking in tongues is necessary. It can be a nice overture to getting in the presence of God and quickly finding peace with reading His Word. Moreover, holding onto a spiritual armistice, like a waving of the white flag, can enable us to receive from God's Word and govern ourselves accordingly as opposed to being faith-based people diagnosed with spiritual atrophy. When under attack, we have to press into God's Word even more as it provides us with the power and authority needed against the enemy trying to steal our joy. I encourage you to do what is working, but if it stops working, then do something different. Dance in His presence, lament for joy in His presence, just sit still in His presence. Sometimes, when I don't know what else to say or do, I just cry out, "Hallelujah." Or just say, "Jesus, Jesus, Jesus," or alternatively, a "Thank You, Jesus," helps to petition me into His presence. He knows we need Him, but looking for that invitation. Or call out to Him, "God, help me," and He always shows up with whatever is needed to comfort me, providing peace, hope, grace, and joy. It brings me back to a place of Eden. Being linked to Him in the Spirit through whatever means possible will help make room for His fullness of joy. A sad and discouraging spirit will not invite joy in. The invitation comes from a receptive spirit. Our spirit longs to connect with Him. Psalm 42:1 (NLT) states, "As the deer longs for streams of water so I long for you, O God." We do have a longing for our creator in proximity, audibly, and spiritually. Cling to His spirit and don't let it go. That's the way to make room for joy. Once your spirit is changed, your thoughts will change, and as your thoughts change, your emotions will change, and as your emotions change, your nature will change, and this will make room for a life change.

Moving over to make room for something new is a progressive process requiring we make room in our thoughts and spirit first before an emotional metamorphosis can happen. Likewise, we also have to move the dissenting emotions out of the way because we cannot hold on to joy and depression at the same time. We need to have the emotional bandwidth to achieve the full reach of emotions for which God has given us the capacity, not just being sad, mad, or angry. He created our emotions as an experiential somatic or bodily process through our five senses as a way to connect primarily with Him, participate and interact with others, and for foresight and understanding in this present world. Remember, we were created in His image and likeness, and God also exhibited emotions from what I read in the Bible. Thus, He created us to have emotions as well. Whenever His anger was kindled against the sin nature of man, this was evidence of His emotions. Additionally, in His pleasure, there were found blessings, a confirmation of the array of emotions that God possessed. We were created with emotions not for them to control us but for us to subdue them. We are not created to be robotic, and that's why we have emotions, an independent thought process, and a spirit that will either align with God or the devil. When our thoughts change to be optimistic and our spirit changes to connect fervently with His spirit, then inevitably, our emotions are going to change. We must move over and make room in our emotions for joy because joy itself is a subjectively pleasurable feeling that draws from feelings that are energetic, enthusiastic, and favorable. For the Christ follower, joy is more than an emotion. It is an empirically religious transaction in response to a spiritually filled lifestyle. We can see this as evident based on the nine pathways to heavenly joy and corresponding scriptures noted previously. Joy is found throughout scripture in consequence to leading a godly life. Now, that doesn't equate to being pompous or thinking of oneself holier than he or she should. None of us are holy and righteous alone except one, and through His bloodshed and our acceptance, we become righteous. There has to be an authenticity to this Christian lifestyle beyond saying you are Christian or in half-hazard demonstrations, principally for the benefit of others instead of the Lord your God. We are to be joyful Christians because we know the final gift is great despite what we may be going through on this earth. This earthly kingdom is not it for us, and as Christ followers, we should know this prophetic fact and live by it. Our joy comes from who we know, not what we own. But if the expectation to live according to the nine scriptures above is correct, then joy is more spiritual than we think and not only an emotional experience. It is a heavenly existence, and we do not have to ascend to heaven to partake of the joy that God has promised us, but we do have to make room for it. You create tangible ways to be cathartic and purgative of these negative emotions that are contrary to the joy God has left you as an inheritance. That joy is available to us now, particularly since scripture is written for the here and now, not for after the coming of Christ, but for preparation of His coming. That type of joy, to which I reference, is evidence of God's existence and a manifestation of our faith in Him. By making room in our emotions, weeding out the old to acclimate to what is new, we enter into that Eden place and a Sabbath rest. No carrying baggage from the past into places that are new. Eden is resourceful, peaceful and transports great provision to us. I only hope that we can all benefit from this joy that is often unspeakable, in many ways miraculous, considering the kingdom in which we currently reside, and certainly inadequately definable by me.

Lastly, making room in our life for joy becomes simple when this successive process is achieved. It's like going up a staircase or climbing a ladder. It has to be one step followed by the next or one rung followed by the next. No one is able to get to the top of a staircase or ladder without going through each stride. The greatest attack against the enemy is living a joyful life through faith despite the distractions from the devil. The circumstances that come up may include lack, stress, disease, discontentment with life, resentments, anger, spousal arguments, evils of all kinds, and all are distractions to discourage us not only from our faith walk with God but from the joy promised to us by God. Do not give in to distractions, whether from a person or our furry friends, and, yes, the enemy will use our pets to come against us as well. I'm convinced of that, as the enemy will use anything at his disposal to steal from us; he is a thief, a liar, and a murderer, the true nemesis to us all. However, if we choose not to give in to these distractions and beguilement and continue to fashion room in our lives for joy, yielding our lives to God by praising Him, we can become the benefactor of this heavenly joy provisioned to us through God.

Chapter 16

The Plot of the Enemy

The enemy is very much trying to steal our joy. The joy that God wants us to have comes from our spirit, not from our soul or our body. It's the spirit because that is what is connected to God. Our joy is a gift from God and part of our inheritance package, so, of course, the enemy wants to defraud us from what is rightfully ours. Why? The enemy is envious of what God has gifted us and that he can never possess. He has a plot strategically designed for each of us to rob us of our joy, abduct our peace, and ultimately destroy the relationship we have with God by making us angry with Him. When circumstances happen that cause us to become angry with God, assuming He didn't hear our prayer, is unwilling to heal, prevents something bad from happening, or has not acknowledged our pain. These things will undoubtedly cause us to become antagonistic toward Him. This is part of Satan's plot to make us think that God doesn't care. I, too, have regrettably been angry with God at times in my life based on various circumstances. I also found that as I maintained that position of animosity toward God, it was like injecting poison into my spirit. It actually anchored my posture of frustration and bitterness, and as I saw my circumstances not shifting, that emotion was transferred toward God as I began to believe the lie that He's not hearing my prayer or doesn't love me as much as He loves so and so. I knew that God doesn't show favoritism as people do; however, I still fell victim to the lie. God would never want wrongdoing for me or any of us. Why pay such a high price for our reunification with Him by giving His only Son just to harm us or want ill for us? Asking myself that question led me back from a path of destruction to falling in love with my God again. When we start thinking contrary to God's Word, it's important to look for evidence of that in God's Word. I couldn't find anything that indicates God wants evil to befall me. On the contrary, I found a plethora of scriptures that publicized God's love for me and us all. The most famous of which is John 3:16, where I camped out for a while until that word sunk into my spirit. God is love, He is good, and He still loves us, in spite of ourselves, He loves us. James 1:17 (AMP) tells us,

> *"Every good thing given and every perfect gift is from above; it comes down from the Father of lights [the Creator and Sustainer of the heavens], in whom there is no variation [no rising or setting] or shadow cast by His turning [for He is perfect and never changes]."*

Every good gift is from our heavenly Father. He is the luminary on this earth, and this gift is indestructible. Since His presence is in the atmosphere for this current season, and every good gift is from Him, then we have to understand that those things that happen to us are not from Him. It's a misconception orchestrated by the enemy to destroy your smile and plant a seed of doubt toward God. We have to jettison the lies of the enemy in our life. That is how we stay victorious and sustain our joy. The Bible tells us that the spirit of a man will sustain his infirmity (Proverbs 18:14). Well, if our spirit is angry and hostile, that is the spirit sustaining and fueling our antipathy toward our situation, toward our God. This tells me that whatever our spirit is feeling will either prolong or mitigate our infirmities, and this doesn't necessarily mean that we have a physical ailment. It could be a distress of the mind, a mental infirmity, or a vexed spirit. You can hold on to that anger if you so desire, but that distress will eventually have an impact on your physical and mental health. Holding anger toward God is a sin, an emotional transgression against our heavenly Father because of how it impacts our behavior toward Him. Unfortunately, none of us see it that way, and so we never stop to think that holding onto anger against God has an impact on us or our conduct. It also impacts our joy in an adverse way since our joy is sourced from Him.

We have a plan from God backed by scripture to know the plot of the enemy. To be aware of how he tries to destroy us, destroy our joy, and terminate our hope in the God of creation. The devil's goal is to cut off our access to God through various avenues. The plot is real, and as long as we are aware of it, that is half the battle. Do not be misled by the enemy when he tries to take your joy hostage and remove your faith in God. Stay strong in believing. Do not commit spiritual adultery by giving up your joy to the enemy. We are asked to rejoice in the face of fear and frustration, as Paul writes in his letter to the Philippians. That is the answer to the enemy's plot: rejoice when feeling melancholy, rejoice when he attempts to manipulate your thoughts, rejoice when he tries to plant seeds of bitterness, seeds of doubt, rejoice when everything he does fails, yet you are still standing. When you start rejoicing, your faith is ignited and helps you stay centered on God. That is the only answer, and the best answer to the enemy's plot is to stay full of joy. Philippians 4:4 (NLT), "Always be full of joy in the Lord. I say it again-rejoice!" The flow of our power in the faith comes from rejoicing. It ruins the plot of the enemy. I encourage you not to be deceived or disillusioned by the enemy. Recognize the plot he has designed for you, which you are well able to overcome.

Chapter 17

Joy Stealers

I can recall a time in my life when anxiety was stealing my joy, the joy I should have had because of my covenant with God. What I have learned is that anxiety has less to do with the things we are worried about and more to do with trust, specifically trusting God. It was the middle of the week on one spring Wednesday when the scripture in Proverbs 3:4–5 continued to flash in and out of my thoughts. Then, on two separate occasions, during my devotional time, Kenneth Copeland and Keith Moore were ministering on the exact same scriptures with a different revelation than God had given me. What was most amazing to me was the revelation knowledge God ministered to me on Friday of that week on how a lack of trust in Him is why so many people suffer from anxiety and fear. It's not about anxiety associated with work, financial issues, spousal problems, etcetera. It has to do with not trusting Him. The aforementioned scripture states, "Trust in the Lord with all your heart; do not depend on your own understanding. Seek His will in all you do, and He will show you which path to take" (Proverbs 3:4–5, NLT). Firstly, I read this and heard a directive that we should trust the Lord. The second directive is that we should not trust our own understanding. And thirdly, seek Him always and in everything. But the education didn't stop there. The Holy Spirit had me read Matthew 6:33 (KJV), "But seek ye first the kingdom of God, and his righteousness; and all these things shall be added unto you." That's when I started to fully comprehend the message the Holy Spirit was sharing with me: to seek Him in everything as that demonstrates trust in Him. As we trust Him, we seek Him, and those who don't trust Him won't seek

Him first. He is eager for us to lean on Him instead of trying to figure things out for ourselves because we don't have all the facts and sometimes can't see the whole picture, particularly if jaded by bias or emotional reactions, such as fear. Fear-based reactions demonstrate a lack of trust in God and reverence toward the enemy and what he is trying to scare you with, which is more of a distraction than the real issue. It is a chance for the enemy to hijack your focus from trusting God. The enemy doesn't want us to understand the real issue underlying the anxiety, and thus the interference and diversions, so you think you're anxious about how to solve a problem at work or getting money to pay a bill, or even the fear of flying or illness. It's not about those secular and primitive things at all. It's indeed about trust. Trust in God has to be our only foundation, as noted in Proverbs 22:19 (MSG). Anxiety and fear are spiritual conflicts and more rooted in darkness than we can possibly discern—that was the message from the Holy Spirit. We have to trust in the one who knows it all. If we trust Him, the creator of our joy, then we do not have to stay in a state of fear. The scripture that tied it all together for me, "See, God has come to save me. I will trust in him and not be afraid. The Lord God is my strength and my song; he has given me victory" (Isaiah 12:2, NLT). Yes, God has come to save us all, but will we be saved, saved from fear by trusting in Him, among the many things that God has come to do? He has given us victory, something to smile about and not be afraid of. But our victory is found by trusting in Him. My question to the Lord was how can I further grow my trust in Him. He brought me to the following scripture,

> *"This book of the law shall not depart out of thy mouth; but thou shalt meditate therein day and night, that thou mayest observe to do according to all that is written therein: for then thou shalt make thy way prosperous, and then thou shalt have good success."*
>
> Joshua 1:8 (KJV)

There are three directions provided in this scripture: confession, meditation, and observance of the law of God. Since then, I have continued to meditate on the scriptures in Proverbs and even the one previously noted in Jeremiah 29:11. God's plans for us are good plans and thoughts for correction, direction, restoration, protection, and good health. He doesn't want us living in a place of fear and anxiety, which is made even plainer throughout scripture. We become enslaved to fear when we live and respond in fear. God's desire is that we have joy, but it's hard to hold onto joy and express it when under the bondage of fear. "For ye have not received the spirit of bondage again to fear; but ye have received the Spirit of adoption, whereby we cry, Abba, Father" (Romans 8:15, KJV). We do not have a spirit of fear for those who are Christ followers because we have been freed from fear through the adoption of Christ in the family of our God. Our spirit in the natural touches God's spirit in the supernatural to liberate us from fear and anxiety so that we can have peace and joy as we fervently seek God's face in scripture and in prayer. The amplified version of the latter half of the above scripture says, "We joyfully cry, 'Abba Father.'" With joy, we can call Him Abba Father when we have been liberated from the bondage of fear. Speak it over yourself that "I am not enslaved to fear, anxiety, trepidations of the flesh, because I do trust God." We are free because we were adopted into the fold, but our trust in Him continues to make us free from fear. Challenge yourself to trust Him and watch the fear be extinguished. This is an example of what our trust in God should look like: "When you pass through the waters, I will be with you; And through the rivers, they will not overwhelm you. When you walk through the fire, you will not be scorched, Nor will the flame burn you" (Isaiah 43:2, AMP). Deliberate that scripture for a little while and identify what it means to you, what you take away from this scripture, and what the enduring promise found in this scripture is regarding your trust in God. We have to hold onto the promises of God as Christ followers. That promise that we do not have to be afraid is captured in scriptures from Genesis to Revelations, and we can hold onto that today. Our body holds onto fear in the form of tension in our muscles or even manifests in the form of headaches or other body aches. I would recommend scanning your body now from head to toe to catalog where you are holding onto fear in your body. Then, concentrate on that diagnosed area of the body where the fear is showing up, and then locate a corresponding scripture to deactivate the fear. Do the same if you scan your thoughts and find that you are holding onto fear in your thought life. Focus on that area and repeat the following scripture by personalizing it, "casting all your cares [all your anxieties, all your worries, and all your concerns, once and for all] on Him, for He cares about you [with deepest affection, and watches over you very carefully]" (1 Peter 5:7, AMP). And continue to repeat this scripture even in the face of palpable fear or symptoms of anxiety. Be joyful about it to demonstrate your victory over fear, then continue speaking this scripture over yourself and praising God until you feel the fear lift, and it will lift as long as you don't give up the fight. Being cognizant of where the fear is landing for you in your body or thoughts will help as biofeedback so you know when the devil is trying to attack you and in what area. It gives you the power to employ the Word of God as part of your counterattack. It's useful knowledge so you aren't destroyed.

Recall the scripture from Matthew 8:23–27, where Jesus is calming a storm. He questions His disciples' lack of faith and assesses it as fear. Faith is trust, so the idea of not trusting God leads to fear is likely defined best by these scriptures. In Matthew 10:26–31, Jesus admonishes against fear while ministering to the disciples. He reminds us that things hidden will be revealed, and those things done in secret will be made known. He knows the number of hairs on our head since God is sovereign. Then, He reminds us not to be afraid of the one who can kill the body only but of the one who is capable of killing the body and the soul. Finally, He compares us to sparrows and reminds us of our value as being greater than they. The point of this parable is to remind us of legitimate discipleship that is decreed to us without fear or retribution. He takes care of us as disciples of Christ just as He cares for the birds of the air. He doesn't want us living in fear or worry since He is able to provide. Fear is punishment and has torment attached to it. There is no peace in fear. It's not God's best and certainly not the plan He has for us. God does not want us trembling in fear regarding whatever situation is coming up at the moment. He wants us to remain divinely connected to Him, and in so doing, we can experience His best joy coupled with peace. As long as we stay in the marriage covenant with God, we take on His abilities, and we put on trust to ward against fear.

On review of a practical example of how to apply the trust of God in a fearful situation, I am going to focus on financial pressure, as it seems to be the theme in some of my sessions lately. I am going to closely look at the famous scripture in Philippians 4:19 that we all seem to focus on and meditate on but may not fully register. They may not see the manifestation of meditating on this scripture. You might be believing God for financial resources for something and holding onto the aforesaid scripture, which reads from the KJV, "But my God shall supply all your need according to his riches in glory by Christ Jesus." Firstly, note that God is our Supplier, as this scripture indicates, recognizing that is pivotal, so our trust is not defined by someone else or placed in someone else supplying for us. God may use other people and occupations as a resource, but He is the supply source. Supply also implies action as a verb, perhaps action on our part as well as God's part, which is explicit in this scripture: He will make supply for us through His virtue and anointing. What is implicit might be the action that has to happen on our part. Moving on, secondly, note that Paul indicates "God shall supply all your need," not plural needs. Have you ever wondered why that is the case? The word proceeding "all" is a description of quantity and an adjective defining the subject "our need." Thus, the reason for not specifying needs is because using the word "all" takes care of that. So, for those who believe that this scripture doesn't speak to all our needs, it does; whatever that need might be, even beyond finances, as long as it is promised through the Word of God, He supplies it. God is not going to supply a need that is not attached to the covenant He has for us because that covenant was established through the purity of Jesus, who was sinless (2 Corinthians 5:21) and sacrificed His life for us (John 3:16). The price was set so high to bring us back in right standing with God, and Jesus paid it, so to not honor the covenant would be to not honor His Son. Then, note that the pronoun "His" in this scripture references God again since that is the noun previously indicated in this scripture, so this promise will happen according to God's riches and glory by Christ Jesus. The "by" tells me that we must have accepted and have a relationship with Christ Jesus in order for this promise to occur. This makes me think of the scripture in John 14:6, "Jesus answered, 'I am the way and the truth and the life. No one comes to the Father except through me.'" It's by Jesus that we access this promise of God being our Supplier. God fulfilling the promise comes by Christ Jesus and our faith in Him. Now that we have gone through the English lesson, a few other components to note about this baseline scripture you might be using for a need you have before God. 1) Don't assume that this is a silver platter situation, and that is the assumption that most take when reading this scripture that somehow our need is going to pour out of heaven into our lap. Where is the supposition for that notion? I think it's based on someone's incorrect assumption that God is going to show up however we need Him, but we have to remember He is sovereign. He is not Santa Claus. God will make provision, but that provision can come in many forms. Sometimes, it's through a silver platter-type situation, such as a door opening for us or an opportunity, but sometimes, it comes through the wisdom of God to refrain from spending money on such and such or going to this place or that where money is needed. On other occasions, the provision could come through the revelation knowledge of God. He does provide us with knowledge for various reasons to do things He's called us to do or make provision in areas where it doesn't seem possible. That revelation knowledge could come in the form of opening a business to be financially successful or where to look for capital for your business venture. We have to stop looking at this scripture as the need will rain from heaven because if we don't see all the avenues in which God could supply, we may miss it and assume God has not answered us, and this might be why we lose trust in Him. Because we don't properly understand scripture, it has an impact on our trust relationship in God. By not trusting, we get into a place of fear again. All that to say, by correctly comprehending scripture and only trusting God, fear is defeated, and our joy is sustained. The whole purpose is to minimize those things that will steal our joy, but trusting that God will fulfill His scriptures makes our joy more full. So you can use the scripture in Philippians 4:19 for whatever your need is, but understand the approaches that He might use without making erroneous assumptions. And while staying steadfast on this scripture or any scripture being used as your baseline for manifestation, exercise the sabbath attitude of rest. The other eight ways to heavenly joy are relevant also, but specifically, staying in rest so we can hear from God through the Holy Spirit is key. We may not always hear if we are constantly distracted. To be clear,

I didn't say to be lazy, which is very different from rest, but resting in God so we can more clearly hear what God is telling us through scripture as He did with me in dissecting the aforesaid scripture. You see, this is the science of the Word for those who assume the Bible is without science. Science is defined as a branch of knowledge or study dealing with a body of facts or truths systematically arranged and showing the operation of general laws (Dictionary.com, 2023). The Bible is the source for the study of theology and is based on the truth, which governs divine laws. Dissecting scripture enables us to interpret God's Word better so we can receive the promises of God's law.

Chapter 18

Trauma and Abuse, the Foundations of Impaired Joy

The devil has declared war against the Christ followers, using the weapons of trauma and abuse as the foundation for spoiling our joy. Through those experiences, he can stream a series of negative emotions, including anxiety, anger, depression, oppression, loneliness, helplessness, hopelessness, regret, hurt, shame, and so on, that adversely affect one's mindset. He uses those tactics to metastasize a spirit of despair in our lives. Think of it this way: If living in the Spirit there is a flow of faith that brings with it more positive emotions, then living in the flesh brings a flow of fear that brings with it more negative emotions. The devil would rather you stay in the latter, but the only way for that flow to happen is through these traumatic, abusive experiences. Trauma and abuse can affect your joy life in ways you may not even realize simply by moving you further away from God. He tries to get you into a place of questioning God's existence, His love for you, whether you are worthwhile, secretly hoping you will destroy yourself. But Romans 5:3–5 (AMP) tells us to rejoice in distress. Don't accept inaccuracies from the enemy. God came in the form of flesh, ministered the Word, died on the cross for our sins, defeated Satan in hell, and rose again in three days so that we could have joy and a reason to rejoice. The mighty hand of God wouldn't do all that for us to live a life of distress. He came to bring us joy, and that joy is everlasting. Trauma is the enemy trying to create infrastructure for where he sees potential. It's a seed he plants, hoping for negative fruit to be produced and rob our joy. It's used to create shame, guilt, sadness, depression, anger, and hostility. It's to subjugate you to your emotions, stopping you from going higher in your faith walk, and enslave you to the enemy's kingdom. We have to understand the greater the potential, the greater the abuse or the trauma experienced. It was to stop you from being fruitful, so he starts early to break you and use that trauma to torment you later. Recognize that trauma has no power over you unless you allow it. That trauma came as a sign you've been earmarked for greatness. I have reflected on my own past trauma and realized that it was the enemy planting seeds of anguish in my life to steer me away from God's plan. He saw greatness from the beginning, so he tried to take me out early, even in my mother's womb, then again at two years old with Kawasaki disease, and again in elementary school with a teacher telling my parents I learned slower and wanted to stigmatize me by putting me in special needs classes. High school was the worst of it, as I was bullied and teased incessantly without any help from teachers or administrators all four years. My support came from the church, and I will always credit my family and pastor equally, the church, and my investment in Jesus, who restores, for saving my life. The trauma didn't stop there, and college brought on new traumas, as did my young adult life that I'm not ready to share, but God knew, He saw, and helped me rebuild along the way. He's still restoring my confidence. The anger I held was only an exterior veneer to disguise the fear and hide my vulnerabilities. The enemy was trying to steal the potential God had predestined for my life, but I had to understand that as the reason why these events happened to me. It was to kill the fruit, the potential, and the esteem needed to do what God had called me to do. Don't think it's a coincidence that trauma was manifested in your life. Ask the "why" to understand the spiritual aspects of the situation. Not, "Why is this happening to me?" But asking, "Why is this happening right now? What is it that God is calling me to do?" I understood why I experienced the torment, to kill the vision for my life for doing exactly what I am doing right now: offering faith-based counseling to others. Yes, we live in a fallen world, yes, there are weeds amongst the wheat, yes, Paul warns of persecution; however, we need to understand the root cause because it's a spiritual attack against you, not just an emotional attack or a physical attack. Whether you grow up in foster care, abandoned by a parent, sexually abused, physically beaten, emotionally traumatized, bullied, and teased, whatever it is you experienced, you have to know that trauma came to take you off of the goal God had for your life because the enemy saw your potential. So, I beg you to take a different view of your traumatic experiences in recognizing that you have been earmarked for greatness. God knows it, but so does the enemy, and now you know it too. You can take some comfort and joy in that. I know this might be hard for some to digest, but everything happens for a reason. It's a spiritual attack, more than one may want to admit. God has created us all for greatness. Some may have positions or platforms bigger than others, but whatever the call is on your life, you need to rise to the occasion. Don't allow the trauma to overpower the call God has on your life. He created us in His image, and His image is great per Psalm 139:14 and Matthew 5:48. So, walk in that greatness no matter what happens because good prevails over evil every time. Don't allow the enemy to take up residence in your life through trauma and abuse. He'll use it to needle you and create further torment if you let him. Remind yourself of the scripture in 1 John 4:4 (KJV), "Ye are of God, little children, and have overcome them: because greater is he that is in you, than he that is in the world." You are great! You are an overcomer! You are greater than what this world has to offer—understand that if you don't understand anything else, your greatness comes from the greater one who lives in you and the one who created you. Your greatness is not found in the place where you currently dwell but in the place where you are going. Don't allow the trauma or abuse to be a point of contention and anger, but view it as a reminder of what you overcame, a badge of greatness, a stamp of approval, a sacrifice of joy.

Chapter 19

Joy Is Our Weapon; It's Worship That Slays Giants

In his book, *A Purpose Driven Life*, Rick Warren describes worship that pleases God as being truthfully accurate, authentically from the heart, thoughtful, not mindless, practical, and rooted in the Word. He further explains that worship is your spirit responding to God's spirit. It involves us delighting in God. Imagine if you worshiped in joy the way Rick Warren described—you would be able to slay giants. It's done in spirit and in truth (John 4:24). If you weren't aware our worship is the best way to experience the joy that God has ordained for us to have during those low moments in life, it is our best defense against Goliath-like problems. Our joy is a weapon for us against the enemy. Not sadness. Not anger. Not resentment, but joy. The devil is looking for ways to come against us and steal our joy, but as we respond with the opposite reaction to what the enemy expects, you actually frustrate him. In the face of frustration, we need to have a well-crafted joy response that slays giants and acts as a shield from the enemy's bitter attacks. Giants are slain when we decide to have a joyful moment in the face of frustration, worry, sadness, or any negative emotions. The next scripture speaks to how to respond as a way to slay giants. It's biblical and not made up by me. James 1:2–3 (NLT) states, "Dear brothers and sisters, when troubles of any kind come your way, consider it an opportunity for great joy. For you know that when your faith is tested, your endurance has a chance to grow." The troubles referred to could be anything that would ordinarily create a pessimistic response from you, but instead, you see it as an opportunity for joy, then respond with great joy. Don't judge your experience. Just enjoy your experience. Your joy moment might look different from another person's joy moment, so you can't compare but recognize these times of being tested as an opportunity for joy. The word "opportunity" could be translated as hope, so troubles actually bring the hope of joy. These adverse situations come as a result to test your faith and determine whose side you are on. Will you choose the God of your salvation or give in to the enemy? Every time he steals your joy, we have allowed him to win. But if we remember that our joy is a weapon, giving God worship, praising, laughing, smiling, and dancing, we are letting God know that we are strong warriors for Him. We are not wimps when we have giant-slaying joy. We honor God with our joy because He is the one who gave it to us. It was earmarked for us from the beginning that true, genuine joy comes from heaven, not this world. As our faith is tested on various occasions and in various situations, your endurance, also known as patience, has a chance to mature. Things that challenge us can help us to grow, but our perception has to be set on the fact that these are growth experiences. I recall hearing about the symptoms of growing pains when I was younger. It comes not only with physical growth—we all go through it as we get older—but also with spiritual growth, psychological growth, financial growth. Those troubles give us an opportunity for growth and joy. Yet, for each opportunity of growth, there might be some pain that coincides with it. But joy has to be your response to the pain, the sadness, the anger, the frustration, or whatever you're feeling. Recognize that you are a giant slayer using your joy to blast the enemy. Your joy becomes like a trumpet to the Lord tearing down the walls and strongholds, similar to the walls of Jericho falling down, as the miraculous story can be found in Joshua chapter 6. Joshua set himself in a position to hear from God during this first battle, defeating the Canaanites with only ram horns, trumpets, and shouts of joy. The Battle of Jericho was won by the Israelites as they, first, followed the instructions given by the Lord and, secondly, because their praise and joy became their only weapon. They didn't doubt what God said would happen, and in the end, they won the battle without using swords, javelins, and ramparts but through the obedience of their joyful worship to God. It could not have been an act that came from human ability but only from God, and that is the formidable force that our joy takes on in the face of confrontation and controversy. When entrenched on all sides, we can bear in mind that our joy demonstrates warfare against the enemy.

Joy has a strength to it that makes it a weapon. That became more clear to me in reading Nancy Dufresne's book, *A Sound Disciplined Mind*, where she explains that rejoicing from the heart releases your faith in God, then God's power is able to meet your faith, and His power creates the change in our circumstances. She goes on to say that "rejoicing holds our attention on God instead of the difficulty, it holds us in the arena of faith. Joy is the fruit of the born again spirit and resident in the believer." That was meaningful to me because joy becomes a powerful weapon when it's released from our spirit, which is the heart of man, and it becomes coupled with our faith. In the dramatic composition of us rejoicing, our faith is fluid. It's the strongest weapon we have when used against the enemy as a source of light for our lives instead of focusing on the problem or the circumstances that we alone may not be able to change. It's God's power that meets us where we are in our rejoicing. That joy we express through singing, dancing, laughing, smiling, praising, or worshiping allows us to go up spiritually toward the direction of God instead of Him coming down to where we are. In essence, He is meeting us where He is. God does challenge us at times to go up to where He is so we can slay giants from on high, a position of our predestined birthright before the fall. From on high is the place where we are licensed to dominate over the enemy. Think about it this way: anything on the bottom is typically not dominating. It's the circumstances or the people on top that dominate. We may not like to hear that, though that's how it works. We were never meant to be on the bottom but to live on top of the world. Our worship should be on top of anything we are facing; it's our demonstration of joy that keeps us aligned with our faith in God, and He's on top. A merry heart is the expectation for the believer as it keeps us on top and becomes a strong weapon in the face of evil. Laughing at the enemy refuels our spirit and becomes worship toward God in our rejoicing. It is a conscious decision you make. It has to be from the heart. It has to be intentional. It has to be meaningful rejoicing for you and to God. It should be our first line of defense. And the best part is that it's practical. We prosecute the devil with our joy and proselyte, showing our full discipleship to God's Word for others in our response to the devil's violation.

He is attempting to violate our peace and joy, but we have the right to hold on to it. Never give up your joy to the devil. It's equivalent to giving up your weapons during warfare. Then, you become exposed and defenseless. We need to maintain our joy at all times, not just during war against the enemy, but it is most useful then. When under attack, it's definitely warfare time, and you need your joy coupled with faith to rise above the attack, letting the devil know his place in your life. He's under your feet! Maintain your joy as a precious gift and weapon that slays giants. Take a moment to laugh or worship or just shout hallelujah in the midst of your situation because the power you demonstrate through that act is your best defense against any attack.

Chapter 20

Stirring Up Lost Joy

How can we stir up lost joy? It's lost because you have allowed the pressure and cares of this world to weigh on you. Or perhaps you have entertained something you shouldn't have or done it unknowingly. Somehow, you gave entree for your joy to be lost. If it's pressure, that comes from the devil because his goal is to steal our joy, kill us, or try to destroy our relationship with God. Actually, it's more accurate to say it's missing joy instead of lost joy for those in the household of faith because our joy is never lost in Christ. If Christ is the center focus of our lives, that joy should be present. You may not be experiencing the fullness of joy God wants you to have as a Christ follower, but that just means something is missing or lacking. Nobody can take your joy from you if you don't allow it. Jesus is ministering to the disciples about the final hours of His life and His plan to go to the Father by providing the following words of encouragement about physically leaving the earth, yet there will be joy left behind that nobody can take away,

> *"I assure you and most solemnly say to you, that you will weep and grieve [in great mourning], but the world will rejoice. You will be sorrowful, but your sorrow will be turned into joy. A woman, when she is in labor, has pain because her time [to give birth] has come; but when she has given birth to the child, she no longer remembers the anguish because of her joy that a child has come into the world. So for now you are in grief; but I will see you*

again, and [then] your hearts will rejoice and no one will take away from you your [great] joy. In that day you will not [need to] ask Me about anything. I assure you and most solemnly say to you, whatever you ask the Father in My name [as My representative], He will give you. Until now you have not asked [the Father] for anything in My name; but now ask and keep on asking and you will receive, so that your joy may be full and complete."

John 16:20–24 (AMP)

While the disciples might have been sad with Jesus leaving the earth physically, this transition to the Father allowed Him to sit at His right hand, the position of authority, acting as our representative to the Father. He is going to make peace with the Father on our behalf, and our acceptance of Jesus provides us with the same authority He has and peace with God. There is more at stake here than we think with Jesus' crucifixion and subsequent resurrection. He defeated Satan in hell before ascending to the Father, making intercession on our behalf with the Father and bringing us back to our true identity with Him. This is why we can rejoice—because He is making a place for us in heaven with the Father. And when Satan returns to heaven to be the accuser of the brethren, Jesus will be there as well, fighting on our behalf as He tells His disciples He will see them again. He will see them again, and we will see Him face to face—another reason to rejoice. God's divine plan was fulfilled, and Jesus became the arbitrator of our blood covenant, bringing us back in right standing with God. The joy is that Jesus is risen and He will return, so for us, Christ followers, our joy is not in this world. It's in our faith through the Jesus covenant, the covenant of grace. He came to fulfill the law (Matthew 5:17). Jesus became an extension of the law through grace. Additionally, Jesus explains that no one will take away from you your great joy because He confirms His plan to return. He doesn't say when, but we know it's going to happen. Then, He tells us to ask the Father and keep on asking that our joy will remain full and complete, as in overflowing and perfect. I did question what we are asking God for, but as I go back to Jesus' ministry, He was teaching, healing, and sharing the wisdom of God wherever He went, all in the name of the Father. This is what we should be asking God for first since the flow of our joy principally comes from being in His will. Nevertheless, per this scripture, you can ask God for anything in the name of His Son. Jesus said the disciples haven't had to ask the Father for anything in my name up until now; however, they are told to ask and keep asking. So, I also believe we can ask for anything and keep asking as long as it's in keeping with His Word. They didn't need to ask the Father since Jesus was present, but I see this as a directive to keep on asking so our joy is full and so that the Father can be glorified through His Son. We can stir up our joy by remembering what Jesus did for us at the cross and the pre-planning that went into it by sharing this assurance via scripture with His disciples. They might be grieving briefly, but eventually, they will rejoice. This also tells me that we may have moments of grief as the disciples experienced during Jesus' arrest; however, our joy can be stirred up again by remembering the bigger picture. Look at your situation and determine what the bigger picture is and how you can stir up joy in that situation. Is that situation being used to execute a bigger goal?

Joy can be lost by position. If you are not joined to Christ, then you can lose your joy. So stirring up joy might consist of moving closer to the Father through the Son. How can you become close to Him? The best way to do so when the flesh is stubborn about moving closer to God is through prayer and fasting. We can fast our way back into closer proximity to God. And using our heavenly prayer language is our direct line of communication to God. If you have fallen away, I encourage you not to give up on your joy. It is yours through Christ, and you have a right to stir it up by re-establishing your connection to the vine. He is the vine, and you are the branch we can't thrive without being connected to the vine. However, if you are in relationship with God through His Son and not experiencing the joy of your faith, then you have allowed the god of this world to rob you in some way. Perhaps you have been robbed through making wrong confessions, constant complaining, or too much exposure to joykillers. Whatever it is, ask the Holy Spirit to help you identify the problem and quickly correct it. If we think about this in terms of the Israelites exiting Egypt, they could not enter the Promised Land, a place of joy, because of unbelief. After all the miracles and signs that

God performed on their behalf, they still didn't recognize God's superior anointing; instead, they doubted Him. In their doubt, they moved out of a right hand position with God into a position of fear absent of faith. Then, they complained about what they didn't have and made negative confessions about dying in the wilderness. They weren't stirring up joy through praise, giving God glory for all He had done in the past, knowing that if He led the Egyptian Pharaoh into seven plagues so that they could be freed from slavery, He could certainly care for them in the wilderness and fortify them to conquer giants. They quickly forgot the miracles that began in Egypt, and in their forgetting, they couldn't stir up joy. They were what Jesus would describe as having little faith. We can easily fall into the same spirit of unbelief and temptation toward God when our desires aren't catered to immediately. The Bible says He supplies all of our needs (Philippians 4:19); thus, we are only left with wants if we apply this principle of God being our supplier in all things. God supplied all their need in the wilderness: light by night, protection from the elements, food from heaven, and so on. Remember, God is sovereign and has ultimate authority, which is demonstrated in all His biblical names. Jehovah Jireh is one—our supplier. The Israelites didn't see God as their supplier, which is evident from their complaints. Instead of taking a position of glory toward God and thanking Him for His mercy and all He had done, they lost hope. If we lose hope, we can also come to a place of losing our joy and not being able to stir it up if we get into a place of unbelief and negative confessions. They made the mistake of hardening their hearts against God. We are cautioned in Hebrews 3:8–9 (KJV) not to harden our hearts, "Harden not your hearts, as in the provocation, in the day of temptation in the wilderness: When your fathers tempted me, proved me, and saw my works forty years." They were provoking, tempting, and denying God's grace toward them. It's a fascinating story to see all that God actually did for His chosen people, and yet they rejected Him. I would also caution you not to harden your heart against God, as that will not stir up joy. However, if we do the opposite of what the Israelites did by welcoming God's grace, giving Him glory and honor, and remembering all that He has done for us in the past, we can stir up joy in our hearts. Joy is stirred up by coming boldly to God's throne, as noted in Hebrews 4:16, that boldness comes from going to God without condemnation and knowing our image in Christ. And as we come boldly before His throne of grace, we obtain mercy and find grace when we need help. The Israelites could have come boldly before God's throne of grace to obtain mercy as well when needed, but with a hardened heart, that is impossible. The most effective way to stir up joy is to recognize God's authority, His righteous power, and ability, remember all that He has done even on the day of trouble, and don't harden your heart. They became joy killers by hardening their hearts through temptation, provocation, and unbelief and then exposed themselves again to the gods of Egypt, worshiping them instead of worshiping the true God of Israel. God requires our worship, and our joy is just an act of us giving Him worship. But to stir up joy, we have to believe first and then act on what we believe by faith. This is only effective for those who are Christ followers because we know that our joy comes from God. The Israelites needed to consider ruminating on what God had done for them in the past. Job quickly recognized his mistake and the reason why he lost everything because of his confessions. He also acknowledged that he needed to drop his complaint when he became upset. We can't complain about what God is doing and expect to stir up joy. Our joy is from Him. Drop your complaints and murmurings and doubts to heed to the one who is the source of your joy. However, those who are not Christ followers likely aren't experiencing joy. They are experiencing happiness. We know this based on the multiple scriptures we reviewed thus far, which state that joy comes from our relationship with God the Father, God the Son, and God the Holy Spirit—the Trinity.

Another way to stir up our joy is by forgetting past dissatisfaction, complaints, and troubles. Job 9:27 (NIV) states, "If I say, 'I will forget my complaint, I will change my expression, and smile.'" This scripture serves as a reference for us when we find ourselves diving into the shadows of darkness and marinating on our complaints and troubles. We need to push past those burdens, forget them, and smile. We need to do exactly as Job is expressing here to forget our complaints. Remembering those things that caused conflict and affliction is not going to birth joy; instead, it gives birth to anger and sometimes fear. If we want to birth joy, then we have to receive the joy-provoking seed, not seed that provokes animosity. Dwelling on our complaints is a negative seed that keeps us from the joy that God has for us. This is why the devil wants us to rehearse the complaints, the troubles, and the dissatisfaction. Everything he does is designed to keep us away from the goodness of God. As I see it, we have the ability to forget our complaints; otherwise, Job wouldn't have mentioned it, nor would the Bible constantly remind us to renew the mind because that also helps us to forget our complaints in favor of smiling. In Matthew 9:14–17, Jesus is talking to the disciples of John the Baptist as they ask him why they don't fast as John's disciples and the Pharisees do. Jesus explains that the bridegroom is with them, but when he leaves, they will need to fast. Then, Jesus goes on to talk about the new wine in old wineskins, verse 17. The scripture from the NIV version says, "Neither do people pour new wine into old wineskins. If they do, the skins will burst; and the wine will run out and the wineskins will be ruined. No, they pour new wine into new wineskins, and both are preserved." New wine can represent many things in this scripture and throughout the Bible. I've always learned that the new wine can be interpreted as the harvest, the joy of God, or the Holy Spirit. Now we know the Holy Spirit came once Jesus left the disciples, as He promised this would happen in John 14:16 and 26. Jesus initially refers to Him as the Comforter. Then, he calls Him the Holy Spirit or Holy Ghost, depending on the Bible translation. So the Holy Spirit could be the new wine coming, and Jesus is explaining that He is with them now as the bridegroom, and when He's taken, they will fast as it brings them closer to Him. Wine was also an important part of Hebrew biblical history. They commonly celebrated with wine, as I see that throughout scripture from the Old Testament to the New Testament. It represented mirth and ripened their joy to drink wine as it showed up at many celebrations. The most acclaimed was the marriage ceremony in Cana of Galilee, where Jesus performed the wine miracle found in John 2:1–12. I am not encouraging people to drink wine; I am simply noting the symbolism during that period in time. I have heard the wine back then had less alcohol content than it does today, so I am certainly not advocating drinking as a way to be joyful. However, during that time, wine washed away sorrow and established joy, just as when Jesus used wine to represent His blood during the last supper, the joy that came from His suffering but brought us life. God was never asking us to do something to achieve joy. He only wanted us to receive joy through following His Word. I already shared several scriptures in God's Word on how to receive joy. I admonish you to meditate on those scriptures. Finally, the harvest, the new wine, could be reflective of anything you are waiting on. Whatever you are expecting to come to fruition is the harvest. Proverbs 3:9–10 (KJV) says, "Honor the Lord with thy substance, and with the first fruits of all thine increase: So shall thy barns be filled with plenty, and thy presses shall burst out with new wine." This scripture is talking about giving, the byproduct of which is the bursting out of new wine emblematic of the harvest. Something new is coming in. So when we go back to our original text in Matthew 9:17, let's look at it this way: the new wine, joy, cannot birth itself in old wineskins, old thought process, habits, and behaviors. The new wine, joy, requires new wineskins, a new or renewed thought process, habits, and behaviors. You cannot maintain distorted thoughts and bad habits and think that you will have joy. Consequently, stirring up joy can occur by substituting the old wineskins for new ones. We all need to self-reflect at times on whether it's time for new wineskins to replace the old. If you need a refreshed sense of peace and joy, determine what needs to change in your life? What old wineskins are you still hanging onto? As a reminder, the Thinking Test is a good resource for such exploration.

Chapter 21

Joy, a Spiritual Blessing

Many people talk about joy as if it's some mysterious, impracticable, and peculiar element, but in fact, it is a spiritual blessing that we find in our union with Jesus and released in our actions and deeds to God and others. Joy is a manifestation of our faith. It's how we survive tests and tragedies. Joy takes berth in the believer's spirit, and we become one with it. We are not expected to be believers without joy. Joy is part of our anointing power. That's akin to having faith without works. Joy is our works, particularly in the face of the enemy. It is our spiritual blessing. Ephesians 1:3 (KJV) states, "Blessed be the God and Father of our Lord Jesus Christ, who hath blessed us with all spiritual blessings in heavenly places in Christ." I choose to believe this scripture is true, and God has blessed me with all spiritual blessings. Biblical inerrancy and infallibility are important beliefs for Christ followers because we recognize the Bible as true and without fault. It's God revealing supernatural truths to us. He is revealing a portion of who He is to us. We have to hold that position so we know the contents of God's Word will come to fruition. There is no joy in contesting God's Word or playing devil's advocate to each scripture that tells us joy belongs to us. Look to the Word of God if you have a joyless life. Nothing in God's Word is said in jest, written for entertainment value, or documented superfluously. Every word has meaning, and we have to choose to believe it. I choose to believe joy is a spiritual blessing for me. Perhaps you should say that to yourself a couple of times. More significantly, this scripture speaks to where the spiritual blessings are found. If we want to experience these spiritual blessings, we have to stay in heavenly places. Our heavenly joy is found in heavenly places. Heaven comes to earth through our spirit, uniting with the Holy Spirit directed by our union with Christ. The Holy Spirit, who was also present from the beginning, has manifested during this dispensation, and we access the spiritual realm through Him as He reveals things to us. Jesus is seated with God in heaven, as will our spirits be if we are united with Him, but they are not physically coming down to us. Nevertheless, we have to go up higher spiritually to meet them. The following scripture explains the process of our union with the anointed one and His anointing leading us to heavenly regions, "For he raised us from the dead along with Christ and seated us with him in the heavenly realms because we are united with Christ Jesus" (Ephesians 2:6, NLT). So, as we stay in the marriage ceremony, we have by proxy access to these spiritual blessings because of Jesus. It is the closest proximity we have to these blessings and may personally experience the blessings by being amalgamated with Jesus. This unity with *Him* allows the Christ in you to be the hope of glory. He lives in us, and we abide with Him if we accept Him. We can stay in heavenly places by authorizing and enabling Jesus to conceive through us His good works and will. We must say, Jesus, it is Your way, Your works, and Your will to be done. It is through the conduit of Christ that we are able to stay in heavenly places here on earth. If we become disconnected from Christ, then we have broken unity, the sacred marriage covenant, with Him and are no longer provided direct access to these spiritual blessings. Joy is a spiritual blessing and comes from above, not from the world or from people or from mysterious actions or from tangibles or from monetary gain, only from above. Paul often made mention of Christ dwelling in our hearts by faith and the profoundness of His love toward us (Ephesians 3:17–19). As we believe in Jesus, we become united with Him in spirit, and He abodes in us, heart and mind. The only contingency is that we must remain rooted and grounded in love. I believe this to mean that we must remain rooted and grounded in Him because He is love. Jesus was the best representation of authentic love that we could ever receive. His love transcends our own weak knowledge, but as we comprehend His love more ardently, we become filled with the fullness of God, and as the Amplified Bible notes, this fullness is the richest experience of God's presence in our lives. I have accepted that the richest experience of God's presence is through

His blessings. He wants us to be flooded with His blessings, but that's a benefit of the sacrament we have with Him through His Son. Christ dwells in our heart per the aforesaid scripture, which is a blessing itself and a cause for rejoicing. But scripture also tells us that every good and perfect gift comes from above, and multiple scriptures point to God wanting us to have joy, so this joy He wants for us is both a gift and a blessing. And it's a good gift. Not every gift we receive from people is a good gift. Some, quite honestly, we might have wanted to return to the store or re-gift, but gifts from God are blessings. It's His favor, mercy, and benefits bestowed on us. If He didn't want us to have joy, His Word wouldn't state it.

> *"May the God of hope fill you with all joy and peace in believing [through the experience of your faith] that by the power of the Holy Spirit you will abound in hope and overflow with confidence in His promises."*
>
> Romans 15:13 (AMP)

Joy is a promise that God wants us to have as part of His blessings to us. His blessings are granted to us forever and cannot be taken away; however, we can move away from Him and thus remove ourselves from the blessing. The blessing only comes in matrimony to His Son, Jesus.

Chapter 22

My Book Notes

These are my notes I began taking while writing this book and then compiled a list on "Practical Ways of Experiencing Joy." Please don't reduce my notes to a script to be followed. Godly joy cannot be diminished to a script. It is by your choice and your relationship with God the Father, God the Son, and God the Holy Spirit that joy is achieved. If you are a Christ follower, joy should already be present in your life. You may not be experiencing it at the intensity, frequency, and satisfying duration you would like; however, it's up to you to determine what is missing to bring the flow of joy to you. Is it rest? Is it a lack of connection to the vinedresser? Is it in what you are entertaining? By reading this book, perhaps you will identify the missing link in your life. This list is meant to be a helpful add-on. Feel free to use this as a way to kick start your journey to the joy Jesus died for you to experience. It's a joy with a constant flow that is everlasting. It should bring a smile to your face and merriment to your heart.

"For I have given rest to the weary and joy to the sorrowing" (Jeremiah 31:25, NLT).

The Flood Treatment:

» **Flooding Yourself in the Bible.** Two ways: reading scripture and praying scripture. Get the Word inside you and use it. You have to maintain a heart of thirsting for the Word of God. God will flood you with what you need from His Word as you thirst for it (Isaiah 44:3).

» **Praise and Worship.** Psalm 150:6, Isaiah 44:23. You can also flood yourself with praise and worship in the act of lifting your hands, kneeling before the Lord, shouting, singing, or dancing. There are seven dimensions of praise and worship. The one most familiar to me is Shabach, as that was the name of my childhood church, meaning "to shout aloud to the Lord." The second most familiar to me is Barak, as the same childhood pastor used to tell us to Barak the Lord during praise and worship service. The others include Halal—"to boast in celebration," Tehillah—"a song or prayer of praise," Zamar—"instrumental worship and rejoicing," Yadah—"raising the hands in thanksgiving for God's mercy," and Towdah—"to express visible thanks or adoration." (Resource: *The Purpose and Power of Praise and Worship* by Myles Munroe, 2005)

» **Spiritual Meditation.** You can flood yourself through godly meditation, a righteous pondering or rehearsing and repetition of the Word of God, a spiritual process that transforms what we believe in an accelerated manner (Isaiah 26:2 and Joshua 1:8). Spiritual meditation can shift circumstances when mental and physical manifestation cannot get the job done.

» **Gratitude.** Flood your journal life and thoughts with what you appreciate, not just thankful for, but truly appreciate in life, your job, your family, your spouse, your children, your home, etc.…If you spend too much time focused on what you don't have, your mind will flow in a negative manner. You lend yourself to a positive flow through your thought life by thanksgiving and appreciation of all that you have or even consider what you are capable of having. There is no sadness in gratitude; it is only joy (1 Thessalonians 5:16–18 and 1 Corinthians 15:57).

The Purging Effect:

» **Renewing and Pruning**. We cannot mistake God's opportunities for the enemy's attack. Opportunities come to build our faith and trust in God. Jesus was the teacher on earth, and as such, every teacher will test their pupils. These are opportunities for us to renew our mind in the Word of God and allow Him to prune the areas in us that aren't producing fruit. Tests are not the same as a demonic attack. It's important to discern the difference so we can smile when we understand that opportunities come to prune us and test us. It helps us renew our faith in God (Isaiah 26:3). God will keep you in perfect peace if your mind stays on Him because you trust in Him. Recognize that our heavenly joy is from God (John 15:1–5). We can do nothing without God. God is the vine, and we the branches. Our joy is rooted in Him. He purges the areas in us that do not bring forth good fruit—a lack of joy. He is also the generator of our purging process and renewing of the mind (Romans 12:2–3). These are some of the things we are to do in Philippians 4:4–9: rejoice in the Lord, be humble, don't be anxious, and think on these things. Things that are lovely, pure, and so on. We are downloading so much garbage every day that we need to renew our mind and let God prune the bad fruit (Proverbs 14:12). There is a way that seems right to man, and the end thereof is death. God is constantly pruning us so that our ways do not lead us to death. God loves us but is always looking for us to spiritually mature. We need His mentality and wisdom to avoid the death trap. That death doesn't have to be physical. It can be spiritual, such as a death in our joy life.

» **Keep Looking Forward!** An act of purging is to look forward instead of behind, purging the past to look into the future. Joy doesn't look behind; it looks ahead. Nobody ever got ahead by looking back (Philippians 3:13–14). Forget those things that are behind and press towards the mark of the prize of the high calling in Jesus Christ. So I strongly encourage you to keep looking ahead. When the mind wants to continually process the past, you must recognize you have the control to stop it. "How?" you may be wondering. Through faithful attention to the cornerstone of your thoughts, the foundation of your beliefs, and the discretion of your speech, you can move forward. Don't go back into the wallows of your mind searching for things that God wants you to purge. Don't be like Lot's wife, who turned her head back when God expressly told Lot to get his family, and don't look back at Sodom and Gomorrah. She turned into a pillar of salt. I often question why she turned her head. Did she not believe what her husband told her would happen? Did she not trust God? Why look back when the goal is to go forward? We have to see what it is in front of us, so we must look ahead to know our next step. This verse speaks about how we should remember to look ahead of our struggles and that the tears we shed today will be like seeds that are planted in a field that, in time, through much toil and suffering, will rise to a great harvest of joy and thankfulness (Psalm 126:5). What you sow in tears you will reap in joy.

» **Walk in Forgiveness.** Did you know that forgiveness is an act of purging? It's the cathartic emotional discharge of past hurts or mistakes from someone else that were inflicted on you. You release the person from a heart-felt vendetta. It's the compassion that God shows us through His mercy by forgiving us. In His forgiveness, He actually wipes the slate clean. He purged our sins. The Bible reminds us that since God has forgiven our trespasses, we should forgive others (Mark 11:25–26). I believe that forgiving and forgetting work in tandem because as you remember something, it won't let you forget. It drudges up the same emotions from that event. Forgiveness helps you purge from the emotional baggage tying you to the past. Forgiveness is the antidote to past hurt as it helps to divorce you from the event that happened and the emotion from that event. In your own forgiveness, you might need to repent. Your own repentance is sometimes how you learn best how to forgive.

» **Watch Your Thoughts.** Your thoughts can be an enemy to your joy life. We have the responsibility of purging our thoughts from adverse cognitive content or dogma that is not serving us well. Your behavior and attitude will follow in the direction of your most prevalent thought. Think joyfully, and you'll be joyful. "Is it really that simple?" you may be wondering. The Bible says in Proverbs 23:7 that as a man thinks in his heart, so is he. What you think influences your behavior, attitude, and choices, ultimately impacting your joy. Many factors influence our thoughts. Let's examine a few: culture, societal mores, politics, our families, morals and values, professional bureaucracy, educational status (formal or informal), and your personal experiences. Some of these influences are extremely negative, such as certain advertisements and news platforms. You are inundated with this rhetoric all day, every day. No wonder you start thinking it's true. Be careful of demonic influences. They are carefully disguised to blind the minds of those who do not believe (2 Corinthians 4:4). The Bible tells us what to think on in Philippians 4:8. That is the prescription to filter your thoughts through when you recognize your joy is waning.

» **Avoid Judgment.** This is two-fold: avoiding judgment of others while also fighting self-criticism, which is self-judgment. Throughout your lifetime, you will need to purge behaviors that are rudimentary and rooted in hate. It's a detestable act, and I know this because the Bible cautions us against it. In Matthew 7:1–6, Jesus is ministering to the multitude when He talks about not judging or you will be judged. He goes on to talk about hypocritical behavior, which rings true because nobody has the perfect life, not in thoughts, actions, ethics, morals, etcetera. In reality, nobody is perfect. You cannot pull the mote out of your brother's eye when you have a beam in your own eye. It's important for us to avoid judgment and even self-criticism because it doesn't lend itself to joyful thoughts or a joyful life. Most people who find themselves in a place of judgment or self-criticism typically are not happy, the man-made manufactured substitute for joy. How can they achieve joy when they can't even achieve happiness?

» **Pursue Your Vision and Dreams.** Many things can consume your vision and dreams, making it hard for you to see the vision and hold onto sacred dreams. It's important to purge those things that pull you away from your vision and dreams. On the path of fulfilling your vision and dreams is where people find joy. There is passion involved in pursuing your vision and dreams, executing something that satiates you as opposed to settling for what is. Your faith motivates you toward the vision, and joy is the byproduct or the end goal. Hold on to your Joseph dreams and maintain your Jeremiah vision.

» **By Faith and Love.** We are expected to walk in love by faith because our faith works by love (Galatians 5:6). It takes faith to walk in love and receive in love. And perfect love casts out fear (1 John 4:18). By love, we maintain our connection to our faith. Faith links us back to our union with God the Father, Son, and Holy Spirit. Love keeps our faith at work. I would encourage you to take the Love Test authored by Pastor Chris Caton, included at the back of the book, if you find that your love is not where it should be. Love brings us back to following the great commandment of God per the New Testament. And when we walk in love, when it takes our faith to do so, we sustain our joy because each time, we are being subjoined with the purest unconditional love from the vine. Remember, our joy is connected to the vine, and using our faith yokes us to the vine. Fear and hate are the opposite of faith and love. The latter, not the first, allows you to find and release heavenly joy since, through faith in love, we are connected to the vine. Being hateful might feel good temporarily when angry or resentful, but it's not the flow of God that will reconnect you to the vine. God created us for attachment, the love part, and for worship—that's the faith piece (Hebrews 11:6). Without faith, we cannot please God. Faith is an important part to this marriage. Sometimes, it takes faith before we can love and receive love in an effort to find our joy. "Put on therefore, as the elect of God, holy and beloved, bowels of mercies, kindness, humbleness of mind, meekness, long suffering" (Colossians 3:12, KJV). To me, this is a demonstration of love. The best example for us of both love and faith is Christ. The best way for us to smile, find, and release our heavenly joy is through staying in a place of love by faith patterned after Christ. "Your kindness will reward you, but your cruelty will destroy you" (Proverbs 11:17, NLT).

» **Fellowship and Deeds.** Fellowship with others or finding connection is so important to living a joyful life. We were created for companionship and attachment, not to be in self-isolation. None of us are expected to be marooned on an island, so it's worthwhile for us to seek out companionship and ways to do good toward others. Fellowship is not just with others but with our Creator as well. We have to walk in the light for proper fellowship with God. Fellowship with God ushers in joy and also causes us to act according to the Word of God. Acting according to the Word of God means not hosting spirits that are ungodly. Certain spirits are not kindred spirits and can cause a movement of negativism. You can't find joy in despondency. Be careful of the spirits you entertain during fellowship, socializing, or whatever name you want to attach to it. The most important is that the spirit is right. Do not be fooled by thinking you are winning them over when, in reality, there is a lingering pessimistic feeling after each interaction. You know the lackluster feeling you might have had after hanging out with someone who is super negative: the derisive and scornful people. The Bible admonishes us not to sit in the seat of the scornful. Why? Because their mood is going to rub off on you. There is always a small transmission that happens because there is a spiritual exchange that occurs during these social events. It's not as innocent as you may think. If you notice your joy is not where it used to be, this could be the culprit. Re-evaluate your friendships. "Don't hang out with angry people; don't keep company with hotheads. Bad temper is contagious—don't get infected" (Proverbs 22:24–25, MSG). In terms of deeds, what we do should be patterned after the Bible and imitate our Creator. Ephesians 5:1 tells us to imitate God and follow His example. I think that says it all. That is the template we should model our deeds after when unsure of what to do or how to approach something. Colossians 3:23 paraphrased says, and whatsoever you do, do it heartily, as unto the Lord and not unto men. You can ask yourself, even in the middle of a deed, if the Lord were present, would you do it that way? Doing good deeds could be a practical way of finding and releasing joy when it's done from the heart, as if you are doing it unto the Lord.

» **Heard Words vs. Heart Words**. The words we hear can influence our behavior, choices, and overall demeanor, which can result in joy or sadness. Be cautious about what you hear because it can steal your joy. If what you hear isn't settling well in your heart, then do not further entertain it. The spirit may not be right. We have to be skillful in staying attuned to the compassionate instruction of the heart instead of what we hear. You have to know when to cut things off, and that might include people. First Samuel 17:11 Saul heard words from the Philistine army, and all became afraid. Each morning, the Philistine giant and army of soldiers came out to taunt the people of Israel. Saul became a coward upon hearing these words, and yet he was considered tall in stature and mighty. He leaned more toward the heard words instead of the heart of who he was created to be. The next three scriptures embody this point well: Proverbs 12:25 (NIV), "Anxiety weighs down the heart, but a kind word cheers it up." Hearing more kind words might be a practical way of receiving joy. Proverbs 4:23 says to guard your heart, for out of it are the issues of life. We have the responsibility of guarding our heart from what we hear. Joy is found in the heart, the part of us that is connected to God—it's within, not from external factors. Luke 6:45 says that out of the abundance of the heart, the mouth speaks.

» **Acceptance of the Grace Gift**. God loved us so much He gave us the grace gift through the sacrifice of His Son. However, there is a choice involved on your part. It's up to you to accept the compassion God is showing us through the grace He provided us. The love He showed us was to bring us back in right standing with Him after the fall of the original first family. At some point, you will have to acknowledge that you can do nothing without Him, and no man comes to the Father except by His Son. It's through Him we receive grace. It's our gift. You are no longer a slave to sin or anything on this earth because grace covers our sins. This gift should not be misused or abused. Second Peter 1:2–9 tells us that grace and peace are multiplied to us in the knowledge of God and Jesus, so that knowledge helps us make a choice to move closer in acceptance of the grace gift or not. If it's multiplied, that means some grace and peace already exist. God has given us everything we need for life, and godliness through true and personal knowledge of Him implies a relationship with Him. He has bestowed on us divine promises. One of those is grace.

» **Giving and Altruism.** Another practical way of experiencing heavenly joy is by being altruistic—giving unselfishly and without an ulterior motive. It's one way for us to imitate our heavenly Father. The Bible says we are more blessed to give than to receive (Acts 30:35). I believe that when Jesus uttered these words, it wasn't just for healing or almsgiving but in all types of giving. Jesus was the true form of altruism. Our giving draws us closer to the Holy Trinity because that is exactly the character and essence of God. He gave to us in unmerited favor, something we could never earn. He gave us His unconditional love in spite of ourselves. He also gave us salvation through the precious lamb of His Son. Then, He gave us the Holy Spirit so we would never be alone. Exercise the use of the Holy Spirit more, for therein you'll find joy. Under the New Covenant, God gave; thus, in our giving, we become intimately allied to the Father, conforming to the image of the Son. There's an intrinsic feeling we can experience that is heartfelt when we are giving and helping others. Second Peter 1:3–9 We are to put on brotherly kindness and to that add brotherly affection, learning to unselfishly seek the best for others and to do things for their benefit—this is the basic definition of altruism located in the Bible. "But since you excel in everything—in faith, in speech, in knowledge, in complete earnestness and in the love we have kindled in you—see that you also excel in this grace of giving" (2 Corinthians 8:7, NIV). We are expected to excel in the grace of giving. "Generous hands are blessed hands because they give bread to the poor" (Proverbs 22:9, MSG).

» **Remain Hopeful**. Having a heart of peaceful endurance ought to help bring a smile to your face. Being hopeful is an act of self-compassion. You are choosing not to be hopeless, wallowing in self-pity, which is not godly behavior. In the last days, we will need to remain more hopeful than ever. Staying in hope might not be a reasonable ask, but it is a feasible task. We must stay hopeful. It helps us to keep looking forward despite our past and despite our circumstances. We have the hope that God does exist, that He has forgiven our iniquities and provides us help during challenging circumstances. There is joy in hope, so stay hopeful. Regardless of what is happening or what will happen, remain hopeful so you can stay in a place of joy. A good way for your hope skill to grow is by reading the Bible every day. It's the best place for us Christ followers to be encouraged. Remember, this is not our final destination. We are only ambassadors for Christ per 2 Corinthians 5:20. We will be reconciled to our heavenly Father, and that should bring everlasting hope. Our citizenship is in heaven, not on this earth (Philippians 3:20).

Chapter 23

Other Practical Ways of Receiving Joy

» **Holding Steadfast to God's Promise.** The promises are the benefits of God. In order to claim those promises, there has to be an alliance with the Father—meaning you have a faithful relationship with Him. How can we claim the promises of God? 1) Acceptance of Jesus as Lord of your life. 2) You have to know what the promises are, so get in the Word and find out what belongs to you. 3) Recognize who you are (image) and whose you are (you are God's special craftsmanship made in His image and likeness). Your image will carry you to the promise, not focusing on your past. 4) Walking according to God's Word and will, using the fruits of the Spirit (Galatians 5:22–23). His word is His will. 5) We cannot be out of the will of God and receive His promises. 6) By faith (Hebrews 11:1–20). 7) Know you have done nothing to earn or deserve the promises; they are God-given. However, the prerequisites include your salvation and being in God's will.

» **Let the Lord fight for You.** Stop trying to fight your own battles. Exodus 14:14 tells us the Lord shall fight for you, and you shall hold your peace. When the Lord is fighting battles for you, then you can hold onto your joy. Why get over into the flesh with anger, frustration, or hate? The fact that God is willing to fight your battles is definitely something to smile about. Romans 12:18 is our commission to live peaceably with all men. I realized the fact that we can live peaceably *if* we allow God to fight the battles for us. The Bible also says vengeance is His, and He shall repay; it is not yours to repay (Deuteronomy 32:35; Romans 12:19). Whatever it is, let it go and let God fight your battles for you. He's got your back! Your job is to maintain your joy. You're in the world but protected from it (John 17:14–16). God loves us, but He is very much a just God. He doesn't exact revenge; however, He will take vengeance as He did with the Israelites when they rejected Him.

» **Expect Persecution and Tribulation.** The Bible warns us about persecutions and tribulations so that it doesn't come as a surprise, yet some folks are still surprised. Make no mistake about it: we are in the last days (Luke 28:8). This is a sign that our Lord is returning. We need to be ready for the persecution and tribulation that is to come, particularly on the church. The enemy is doing what he can to move those who are on the fence or those who are not as secure in their faith to His kingdom. He's trying to scare you away from the things of God, but don't be afraid. What he may have in power, we make up for in authority and reverent wisdom. Preparation is key during this time. Don't fall for every shiny, extravagant thing. It could be a wolf in sheep's clothing. It may look good, but it may not be right for you. Part of your preparation comes from knowing who you are in Christ and the covenant you have with God. He provides divine and angelic protection so all the heavenly hosts are acting on our behalf in every domain to protect us from the enemy's devices. You have spiritual tools you need to be using. The enemy can't touch you unless you give him access. The challenging times are upon us and even greater to come, but worship your Lord, stay joyful, showing a smile in the face of adversity as a way to push the enemy back. Romans 12:1, AMP version, reminds us that presenting our bodies is an act of worship. We can worship God as a living sacrifice simply by how we present our bodies to Him, including our facial expressions. Smiling and laughing in the face of the enemy is your act of worship to God. It lets the devil know your position is immovable and transfixed on solid ground. Rejoice, for God is with you. "Be on your guard; stand firm in the faith; be courageous; be strong " (1 Corinthians 16:13, NIV). The last days are approaching (2 Timothy 3:1, 1 John 2:18). Are you prepared?

» **Safety and Security**. As we feel safe and secure—also a psychological need, not just physical —it can increase our joy. When folks are fearful and anxious, how can they take joy in their distress when feeling insecure and unsafe? It's tough to do so. Fear is oftentimes the biggest roadblock to our joy. But it's not really about the fear itself. It's about trust. More specifically, trust in God, as we discussed previously. We may not be able to manage every situation to create safety and security; however, whatever is in your control to do, do it. And what is not in your control, leave the rest up to God. Trust that He will see you through. It may seem tough-minded to feel safe and secure considering the political crisis in our country and around the world, the rigidity of systems trying to subjugate Christians, and the chaos happening. But don't grasp safety with your mind. Grasp it with your faith and trust that whatever happens economically, in society, or around the world, you are protected. Don't look at the things seen but the things unseen. I know some are thinking, "How could God really protect me?" If you ever had a near miss in an accident or possibly been in an accident where you could've been seriously injured, yet you weren't. That was God. Or maybe He showed up on your injury or sick bed after an incident. He's protecting your body from death.

> A lot of my safety and security is rooted in my faith in God. God is able to keep us safe and secure as we remain in the perfect will of His plan for us! I have to understand and take heart in God's promise to keep me safe and know that this is evidence of Bible prophecy being fulfilled when I stay within the framework of His plan for me. Trust God more with your safety, and your joy will increase; the only caveat is not to deviate away from His plan for you.

Second Corinthians 9:6–8 says if you sow sparingly, you will reap sparingly. As true believers of Christ, we are expected to abound in every good work. Sharing a smile is a good work. This is the opportunity for us to thrive in every good work. I want a bountiful harvest, so I am always sowing in all ways and always. Stay fruitful as God has licensed us to do. By staying fruitful, you won't have time to be sad.

Joy is a posture of the heart. We maintain our joy by staying in a place of being righteousness-conscious, not sin-conscious. We are the righteousness of God in Christ Jesus (2 Corinthians 5:21), not because we are right but because He was right. Remembering this doesn't allow the enemy to lord past sins over you. He wants to accuse you by making you feel less than, less confident, or less worthy. But you are worthy because of the high price Jesus paid sacrificing His life for you. I recall hearing years ago that it's not the value of the merchandise that is important but the sacrifice made that makes the merchandise worth any value. We are the merchandise, and Jesus was the sacrifice. Our joy isn't only a gift from God but a payment made on our behalf so the enemy cannot accuse us or steal from us based on our past mistakes. How can he steal our joy? It's through our thoughts. He can intercept our thoughts by inserting himself as the accuser, holding us accountable for past mistakes and missteps. He cannot interpret our thoughts, so when he tries to steal your joy, recognize you are in right standing with the Father. It's a place he will never be able to step into, so he is jealous of you. For all the evil the devil has done, he is looking to project his sins onto you, yet he is the biggest sinner of all. Don't accept that displaced transgression. Do not take it to heart when he tries to come back to accuse you of something you did ages ago. Let it go because God has, and your joy is tied to pressing forward, not looking back. You have been redeemed and cleansed by the blood, so you are a new creation. The old is passed away, and behold, all things are new (2 Corinthians 5:17). If that's not something to smile about, I don't know what is because it's such a beautiful thing to be on the edge of a horrifying fate, yet be ransomed back by God and made a new creation. If you haven't smiled yet, I would suggest you take time to smile. It is honoring to God when you connect with scripture in such a powerful way.

You have to work on grasping with your spirit, not your mind, that you are the righteousness of God in Christ. The only real way to do that is to meditate on those scriptures that speak to your spirit about being forgiven and reminding you of your position in Christ with the Father. You can't do anything to change that once you claim Christ as Lord of your life. If you happen to fall, that is what the Holy Spirit is there for to help pick you up and make things right again. Repent from your error as soon as you're aware so the devil doesn't use that as power over you. You don't need the enemy lording your sins over you, as that is an avenue for stealing your joy. Once you repent, recognize quickly that you are the righteousness of God in Christ. You are not condemned because there is no condemnation in Christ since the law of the life-giving Spirit has freed us from sin (Romans 8:1–2). As you confess your sins, it results in God being faithful and just to forgive your sins and cleanse you from all unrighteousness. This next scripture is a reminder of our standing with God. Psalm 23:6 (KJV) states, "Surely goodness and mercy shall follow me all the days of my life: And I will dwell in the house of the Lord for ever." Wherever you go and whatever you do, goodness, the joy of God is following you, and if you transgress, His mercy is enough to provide you with clemency, a compassionate grace that only He can give. This is not a license to sin, as many ministers have already stated. It's to avoid oppression from Satan so you recognize he is not your master. When you get saved, you take on God's nature and become the righteousness of God by Christ Jesus through faith. Once you understand how much God loves you, you will want to change your behavior, which occurs over time by way of sanctification. We are not under the law but under grace (Romans 6:14), and grace, like joy, is a gift from the Father. Both function in tandem. Under grace, we can receive heavenly joy.

You are worthy of this gift of joy as you stay under the New Covenant. The Old Covenant will be a reminder of your sins because of the law, so you remain conscious of your sins. The Bible says, "My people perish for a lack of knowledge." They are lacking insight as to who they are in Christ. Understanding your identity in Christ is a huge part of accepting this heavenly joy as a gift. You don't earn it. Everything from God was already given to us. He has given us everything pertaining to life and godliness (2 Peter 1:3), so we already have it. It's up to you to receive it. Some people aren't living in the fullness of joy God promised them, but that's why it's important to measure your life against the Word of God. Figure out what is missing. What do you need to change? What are you not doing or doing enough that you should be doing? What is the Holy Spirit ministering to your heart?

I leave you with these scriptures, one to both smile about and to see joy in it.

> *""Hey there! All who are thirsty, come to the water! Are you penniless? Come anyway—buy and eat! Come, buy your drinks, buy wine and milk. Buy without money—everything's free! Why do you spend your money on junk food, your hard-earned cash on cotton candy? Listen to me, listen well: Eat only the best, fill yourself with only the finest. Pay attention, come close now, listen carefully to my life-giving, life-nourishing words. I'm making a lasting covenant commitment with you, the same that I made with David: sure, solid, enduring love. I set him up as a witness to the nations, made him a prince and leader of the nations, And now I'm doing it to you: You'll summon nations you've never heard of, and nations who've never heard of will come running to you Because of me, your God, because The Holy of Israel has honored you.""*
>
> Isaiah 55:1–5 (MSG)

""Come to Me, all who are weary and heavily burdened [by religious rituals that provide no peace], and I will give you rest [refreshing your souls with salvation]. Take My yoke upon you and learn from Me [following Me as My disciple], for I am gentle and humble in heart, and you will find rest (renewal, blessed quiet) for your souls."

Matthew 11:28–29 (AMP)

"Repeat these basic essentials over and over to God's people. Warn them before God against pious nitpicking, which chips away at the faith. It just wears everyone out. Concentrate on doing your best for God, work you won't be ashamed of, laying out the truth plain and simple. Stay clear of pious talk that is only talk. Words are not mere words, you know. If they're not backed by a godly life, they accumulate as poison in the soul. Hymenaeus and Philetus are examples, throwing believers off stride and missing the truth by a mile by saying the resurrection is over and done with."

2 Timothy 2:14–18 (MSG)

A Prayer of Salvation

John 3:16 (KJV) states, "For God so loved the world, that he gave his only begotten Son, that whosoever believeth in him should not perish, but have everlasting life." Dear heavenly Father, I am a whosoever believing in You, and thus I know I will not perish but have everlasting life. Romans 10:9 (NIV) states that If I declare with my mouth "Jesus is Lord" and believe in my heart that God raised Him from the dead, I will be saved. Right now, I confess that Jesus is Lord and the Lord of my life. I believe that He was raised from the dead. He has taken my sins on the cross, and so I am justified to the Father because of His sacrifice. Thank You, Father, for forgiving everyone of my sins as Your Word says if I confess my sins, You are faithful and just to forgive my sins and purify me from all unrighteousness (1 John 1:9, NIV). The Bible also reminds me that I can substitute my darkness with His light,

> *"This is the message we have heard from him and declare to you: God is light; in him there is no darkness at all. If we claim to have fellowship with him and yet walk in the darkness, we lie and do not live out the truth. But if we walk in the light, as he is in the light, we have fellowship with one another, and the blood of Jesus, his Son, purifies us from all sin."*
>
> 1 John 1:5-7 (NIV)

Thank You, Lord, for helping me to walk in the light. I pray, Father, that You regenerate me by the power of the Holy Spirit and that He will come to abode in my life, helping me to walk morally according to Your Word. I receive my salvation as a gift from You and thank You, Father, for saving me, Amen.

If you said this prayer in earnest and plan to follow through, make a formal attestation by signing your name below and dating it. It will also act as a reminder of a significant date in your life when you decided to give your soul to the Lord.

____

Print Name

____

Signature

____

Date

A Prayer for Joy

Dear heavenly Father, Your Word states in Job 22:28 paraphrased that I shall decree a thing and it shall be established and His light shall shine upon my ways. I decree I have heavenly joy right now in Jesus' name and ask that You, Father, continue to shine Your light upon the pathway of my life. Help me to smile when I am not feeling like I can in the natural. Help me to walk in the fruits of the spirit where joy resides. Help me to recognize I am the righteousness of God in Christ. I will stay in Your presence, for there is fullness of joy there. I will stay in a place of Sabbath rest. I delight in honoring Your commandments. I ask that You help me not to entertain material or persons contrary to this gift of joy God orchestrated especially on my behalf. I pray, Father, that You saturate me with Your unspeakable joy. I recognize God as the giver of my joy through my salvation and the redemption that I have in Christ Jesus. This makes me heirs with God and joint heirs with His Son, Jesus (Romans 8:17). Now I have become linked to the vine and the vine-dresser, bringing me into closer proximity with You to bear good fruit. I am grateful to have an intimate relationship with You that brings me into deeper fellowship so that I hear from You on accessing my heavenly joy. I praise You, Father, forever for the joy that I have received because of Your love. My joy is complete in You. From this day forward, I choose joy over any of my circumstances, sadness, and fear. I ask that, through the power of the Holy Spirit, I be encouraged to remember my heavenly joy in the midst of challenges. The joy of the Lord is my strength (Nehemiah 8:10), so I can be strengthened to do anything as I remain joyful. All this I pray in Jesus' name, Amen.

My Declaration of Joy

As a way of responding to the information you learned in this book, I ask that you consider authoring your declaration of joy. What do you plan to include as part of your declaration? The nine aforementioned avenues using Bible scripture are not steps for finding and releasing your joy, yet they provide some direction for us on what we need to do both spiritually and physically. Perhaps consider what scriptures you plan to incorporate as part of your declaration. There are a plethora of scriptures in the Bible referencing joy, so you don't have to be restricted to the scriptures mentioned here. Be led by the Holy Spirit regarding the scriptures He's leading you to do since God's Word is not just a good read, but it's active. Use the space below to write your declaration of joy in faith. Don't be a spectator. I encourage you to be a participant in your joy life and engage your declaration now. Take time to smile to others and yourself not just as a hobby but as a practice!

The Thinking Test

Philippians 4:6-9

Philippians 4:6-9, Be anxious for nothing, but in everything by prayer and supplication, with thanksgiving, let your requests be made known to God; 7 and the peace of God, which surpasses all understanding, will guard your hearts (emotions) **and minds** (thinking) **through Christ Jesus. 8 Finally, brethren, whatever things are true, whatever things are noble, whatever things are just, whatever things are pure, whatever things are lovely, whatever things are of good report, if there is any virtue and if there is anything praiseworthy—meditate on these things. 9 The things which you learned and received and heard and saw in me, these do, and the God of peace will be with you. NKJV**

Are your thought-life and emotions giving you trouble? Do you lack peace in your life? Then **do something** about it! Run yourself through "The Thinking Test."

Ask yourself the following questions to locate yourself. Determine what changes need to occur. Remember, as a Christian, you have the mind of Christ (**I Corinthians 2:16**). That means you have a strong mind. You have a peaceful mind. That means you have power and control over what you think about.

Yes	No	
O	O	Have I been anxious about anything?
O	O	Have I prayed? Have I talked to God about my problem?
O	O	Have I supplicated – that is, have I earnestly asked God to do something for me? Have I made a definite request of Him?
O	O	Have I thanked God for meeting my need (after I've asked in faith)?
O	O	Have I done Verse 6? I can't expect to receive the benefits of Verse 7 without doing Verse 6 first.
O	O	Is the thing that I am thinking about true / truthful?
O	O	Is the thing that I am thinking about noble / honorable?
O	O	Is the thing that I am thinking about just?
O	O	Is the thing that I am thinking about pure?
O	O	Is the thing that I am thinking about lovely?
O	O	Is the thing that I am thinking about a good report?
O	O	Is the thing that I am thinking about virtuous?
O	O	Is the thing that I am thinking about praiseworthy?
O	O	Have I learned anything from the spiritual leaders in my life?
O	O	Have I received anything from them?
O	O	Have I heard and seen anything in their example?
O	O	Have I been DOING the things that I have learned, received, heard, and seen from my spiritual leaders?

The Love Test

1st Corinthians 13:4-8 (AMP)

Are you having conflict with someone? Then **do something** about it! Run yourself through "The Love Test." Check off the **1st column** if you have no problem in that area. Check off the **2nd column** if you find a trouble spot. **Be honest** and get excited because God is about to talk specifically to **you**!

After taking "The Love Test," **repent** where necessary, **commit** to obey God's Word, and ask God what **actions** He wants you to take to make things right. **Please remember** that "The Love Test" is a **self-test only**. Don't attempt to run anyone else but yourself through it.

1st	2nd	
O	O	Love endures long,
O	O	and is patient,
O	O	and kind;
O	O	love never is envious,
O	O	nor boils over with jealousy,
O	O	is not boastful
O	O	or vainglorious,
O	O	does not display itself haughtily.
O	O	It is not conceited,
O	O	arrogant,
O	O	and inflated with pride;
O	O	it is not rude,
O	O	unmannerly,
O	O	and does not act unbecomingly.
O	O	Love, God's love in us, does not insist on its own rights
O	O	or its own way,
O	O	for it is not self-seeking;
O	O	it is not touchy,
O	O	or fretful,
O	O	or resentful;
O	O	it takes no account of the evil done to it,
O	O	it pays no attention to a suffered wrong.
O	O	It does not rejoice at injustice and unrighteousness,
O	O	but rejoices when right and truth prevail.
O	O	Love bears up under anything and everything that comes,
O	O	is ever ready to believe the best of every person,
O	O	its hopes are fadeless under all circumstances,
O	O	and it endures everything without weakening.
O	O	Love never fails,
O	O	never fades out,
O	O	or becomes obsolete,
O	O	or comes to an end.

Afterword

So what do you say now that you have thoroughly read this treatise on joy—this blueprint for having, walking, and living in God's heavenly joy?

Do you now feel the inward spiritual strength this teaching and encouragement has worked within you? Are you not prepared, equipped, and now ready to eradicate the subpar, second-rate, and substandard world of sadness that tried to characterize your existence in the past? Do you not recognize the supernatural presence and anointing of the Holy Spirit upon and within you now, beckoning you upward into the power and provisions of your Lord Jesus Christ to propel you forward in God's foreordained purposes for you being here on this earth and you being a member of God's family at such a time as this?

I'm sure you do sense all of this! I'm sure you are now aware of some things about yourself, your God, and His provision of Joy that you never saw before!

So *rejoice*! Because you have been *ruined* for ever going backward into the former days of darkness!

Rejoice! For though challenges and conflicts may still exist and may still come, you have the spiritual weapons to overcome and *win*!

Rejoice! For the glory that *is* upon you right now, and for the glory (the heavy with everything good of God) that will continue to be revealed to you as you walk and live out these truths that shine brighter and brighter until He comes!

So take your joy and clothe yourself with your anointed smile!

Contribution by Rev. Christopher Caton

References

Capps, C. 1987. *Faith and Confession. How To Activate The Power Of God In Your Life*. Broken Arrow, OK: Capps Publishing

Dictionary.com. 2023. "Science." https://www.dictionary.com/browse/Science.

Dufresne, N. 2011. *A Sound Disciplined Mind Living Free From Worry, Fear, Depression & Doubt*. Murieta, CA: Published by: Ed Dufresne Ministries.

Levine, C. M. 1997. Obedience. Random House Webster's College Dictionary, 2nd ed.: 627. Random House, Inc.

Merriam-Webster (n.d.). Joy. Merriam-Webster online dictionary. Retrieved September 24, 2022, from https://www.merriam-webster.com/dictionary/joy

Merriam-Webster (n.d.). Sweet. Merriam-Webster online dictionary. Retrieved December 4, 2022 from https://www.merriam-webster.com/dictionary/sweet

Munroe, M. 2000. *The Purpose and Power of Praise and Worship*. Shippensburg, PA: Destiny Image Inc.

Smith, M. 2002. Th*e Power Of The Blood Covenant – Uncover The Secret Strength In God's Eternal Oath*. Tulsa, OK: Harrison House, Inc.

Warren, R. 2002. *The Purpose Driven Life. What On Earth Am I Here For?* Grand Rapids, MI: Zondervan.

Whitefield, S. 2020. *Have You Been Blinded? Facing Your Assumptions About God's Leadership*. Grandview, MO: OneKing Publishing.

About the Author

Charlene Moorer is a national board-certified and licensed professional counselor with a graduate degree from Pace University and a private practice in Connecticut. She is also a board-certified Christian counselor as of spring of 2023. She has been practicing in the field for over twenty years in various capacities and positions. She is devoted to the field of psychology and the humanities, serving hundreds of patients at her practice—CDM Counseling & Consultation Services, LLC. Her work with youth and families as the former program director at The Bridge Family Center inspires her work in practice and, coupled with her current vocation, prompted the writing of this book. She also runs a small spiritual and Bible study group with co-facilitator Maria Cavaiuolo. When she is not working, she dedicates time to her family, maintaining positive self-care, and engaging in philanthropic efforts. To learn more about the author, you can find her on LinkedIn or visit her website: https://cdmcounselingllc.com.

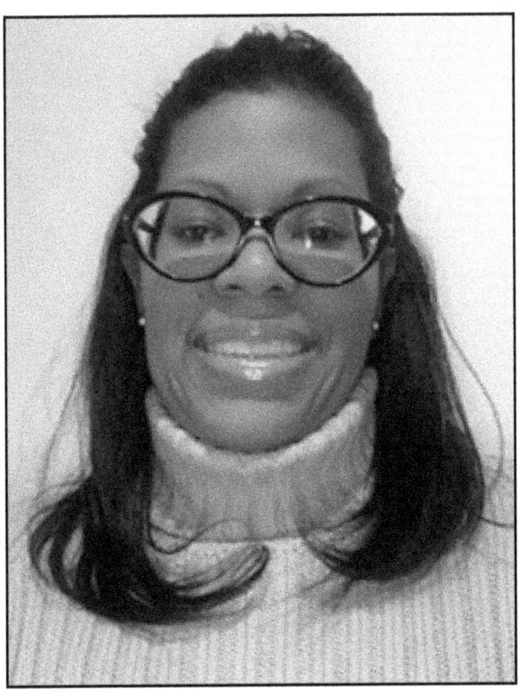

Milton Keynes UK
Ingram Content Group UK Ltd.
UKHW030905141024
449705UK00012B/555